AMERICAN
WOODWORKER™

THE WOODWORKING SHOP

 Rodale Press, Emmaus, Pennsylvania

Printed in the United States of America on acid-free paper containing a high percentage of recycled fiber.

Library of Congress Cataloging-in-Publication Data

The Woodworking shop
        p.   cm.
    At head of title: American woodworker.
    Includes index.
    ISBN 0-87857-794-7 paperback
    1. Woodworking tools.   I. American woodworker.
TT186.W66   1989
684.08 – dc19   88-29349
                                                          CIP

2   4   6   8   10   9   7   5   3   1   paperback

Contents

HAND PLANES

by W. Curtis Johnson

Photographs by the author.

I find planing with a well tuned hand plane the most exquisite joy in woodworking. Last summer I shared this joy with the people of Corvallis, Oregon at our annual Imagination Celebration. I invited everyone who passed the workbench, set up on a downtown sidewalk, to try hand planing. Children and adults alike were delighted to shave a thin slice of wood from the edge of a board. Most people took a treasured, curly shaving with them. In this series of four articles, I hope to convince readers, who are wedded to their machines, to try hand planes. Performing many tasks more easily and better than machines, hand planes are not difficult to use if they are first tuned and sharpened. In this article, I will discuss the planes I find particularly useful. In future articles, I will cover tuning hand planes, sharpening plane blades and similar edged tools, and finally, the use of hand planes.

I have quite a collection of hand planes, but when I think about it, there are really only four that get a lot of use. My workhorse is the Record No. 05 jack plane. The Stanley No. 60½ is a low-angle block plane which is useful for trimming with one hand. The Record No. 073 is a rabbet plane, which removes thin shavings from the face of tenons and smooths their shoulders for a perfect fit. The finger plane gives good control when trimming small projections, such as exposed splines in a miter joint.

My jack plane has a 2 inch wide blade and is 14 inches in length. With it, I can quickly flatten rough cut lumber, true the faces, and smooth it by removing thin, translucent shavings. I can plane edges so that the joint between two boards will have an invisible glue line. If you are a beginning woodworker with only a table saw, this is the tool that will allow you to progress beyond plywood and use solid wood for your furniture. If the jack plane is tuned and sharpened as described in the accompanying articles, it is really quite easy to use.

Before mechanical planers were available, four different "bench" planes were generally used for preparing lumber. A scrub plane of moderate length has a flat bottom

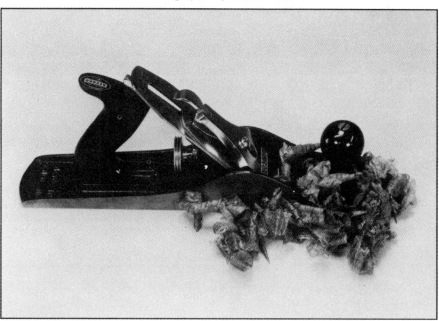

A hand plane will flatten and smooth a wooden surface quickly, yielding delightful, curly shavings.

but a somewhat convex blade. It quickly removes large amounts of stock when used diagonally across the board. Today even rough cut lumber is reasonably flat, and if you do not have a planer, you are probably buying lumber that has its faces surfaced anyway. In the rare circumstance that you need to remove large amounts of material, set the blade of your jack plane for a deep cut and plane diagonally across the board. It will make short work of the task. The jack plane is used to make the faces fairly flat. Actually, the modern jack plane is fairly long, and I find that it produces a face that is true enough so that a long jointer plane is unnecessary. A short smoothing plane is meant to remove extremely thin shavings and put the final surface on a board. I find that my jack plane will do this just fine if the blade is sharp and set for a minimum cut.

Some professionals recommend a smoothing plane (like the 10 inch No. 04) and a jointer plane (like the 22 inch No. 07) over the jack plane. That's probably good advice, but it almost triples the investment to get started. I have been able to plane short boards with my jack plane, but I did finally buy the smoothing plane because it is less cumbersome.

Wood or metal planes present another choice. I prefer the metal planes, shown here, to the wooden planes I own. True, the metal planes are heavier to move, but that weight helps keep them on the board. Your hands are closer to the surface of

Exceedingly thin shavings can be produced by a well-tuned hand plane with a sharp blade.

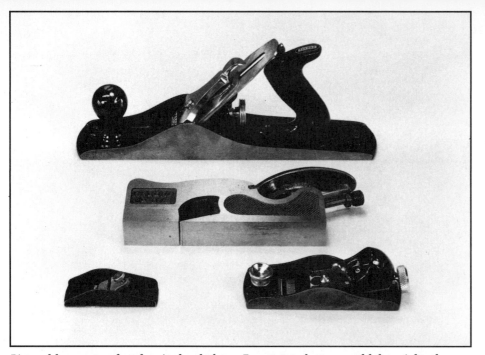

Pictured here are my four favorite hand planes. From top to bottom, and left to right, they are: a Record No. 05 jack plane, a Record No. 073 rabbet plane, a Stanley finger plane, and a Stanley No. 60½ block plane with a low angle blade.

smooths end grain just fine.

The hefty No. 073 is an expensive plane but one well worth the price. For your money, you get a precisely machined tool that needs no tuning except to narrow the blade to the width of the body. Of course, the blade should be polished on the flat side and sharpened. This rabbet plane is useful whenever you need the edge of the blade to be flush with the side. As expected, it nicely smooths rabbets, but I use it regularly to cut the last thousandth off an oversized tenon.

The little finger plane was a Christmas gift from my young son, who was excited to have found a plane in his price range. I use it all the time for trimming where even the block plane is unwieldy. The plane is too small and basic to need tuning, but again, the blade must be polished on the flat side and sharpened.

These are my favorite planes, and I don't know what I would do without them. They allowed me to make a lot of furniture before I owned many

the board with a metal plane, and I find this less cumbersome. It is also true that the wooden planes slide better, but the metal planes will slide equally well if you periodically rub a little paraffin (an old candle stub will do) on the bottom. Furthermore, the sole of a metal plane stands up better against abuse, like planing the glue line when some glue still remains on the surface.

Japanese planes are popular now. These laminated blades are meant to be pulled and are valued for the thin shavings they produce. I have no experience with Japanese planes, but any choice is a trade-off. Japanese planes also have a wooden body and must be adjusted by tapping with a hammer. Certainly when the blade in my well-tuned plane is sharp, I can produce exceedingly thin shavings which I suspect are as thin as those produced by any Japanese plane. Also a variety of blades is now available for western planes, including laminated ones.

The compact block plane fits nicely into one hand leaving the other free to hold the work. It is very convenient for all trimming as well as rounding

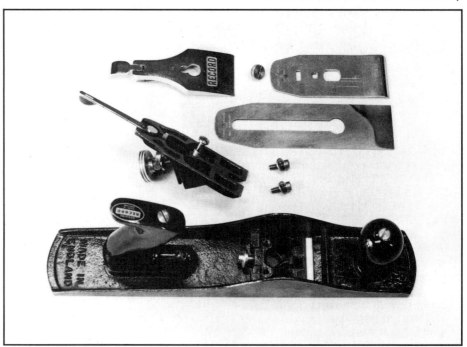

The parts of a metal bench plane. From top to bottom, left to right, they are: lever cap; cap iron or chip breaker with the screw that holds it to the plane blade; cutting iron or plane blade; frog with the screw for securing the lever cap; the mechanism for adjusting the depth of the blade; the lever for straightening the blade, and the screws that hold it to the body; the plane body with the handles; the adjusting screw for the frog; and the mouth through which the sharp edge of the blade protrudes.

edges. The low angle of the blade sheers end grain nicely, but again there is a trade-off. This sheering, combined with the lack of a chip breaker in block planes, is likely to cause tear-out when planing with the grain. Thus, if I were buying a block plane, I'd buy the standard angle No. 9½. The 20° angle that the blade on this plane makes with the sole, plus the 25 to 30° from the up-turned bevel, gives a net angle of 45 to 50°. This is comparable to the 45° angle that the blade makes with the sole in most bench planes where the bevel is down. The larger angle gives more of a scraping action that is less likely to cause tear-out. Use the adjustable mouth to narrow the opening. This will help to prevent tear-out and partially make up for the lack of a chip breaker. How about planing end grain with the larger angle? My jack plane

power tools, and today I use them with superior results, to finish what my power tools only started.

About the Author:
W. Curtis Johnson is a contributing editor to **The American Woodworker.**

Using Hand Planes

By W. Curtis Johnson

When edges need to be precisely perpendicular to faces, I clamp a simple device to my plane. The 9 inch by 3½ inch plywood creates the right angle. Two pieces of ¼ inch hard board that are 9 inches by 1¾ inches are glued to the plywood to move the blade ½ of an inch and over the board.

PHOTOGRAPHS BY THE AUTHOR

Hand planes are a joy to use if they are well tuned and the iron is sharp. The first three articles in this series discussed the four hand planes I have found most useful, how to tune them, and how to sharpen a plane iron so it will shave. Here we will see how hand planes can be used to improve the results of using power tools alone.

Begin by adjusting the razor sharp iron. Center it in the mouth and back it off so the edge is just below the sole. The edge must be precisely parallel to the sole, and this is easily done if the mouth was filed accurately in the tuning process. Hold the plane up to the light and sight along the sole from back to front. You will see the shiny edge of the blade, a dark shadow from the interior of the mouth, and the shiny sole. Using the narrow shadow as a guide, adjust the edge of the blade so that is is parallel to the edge of the mouth. Most bench planes have a lever to facilitate this adjustment, but you will have to push near the end of the blade itself on other types of planes.

Most planes move the blade with some kind of adjusting nut. Put a scrap of wood in your vice and plane an edge along the grain while slowly adjusting the blade further out of the mouth. Stop when the blade cuts a paper thin shaving. Back off the adjusting nut so there is only slight pressure or the blade will slowly creep forward. Plane with each side of the blade to test if the edge is parallel to the sole. For simpler planes, like my finger plane, put the sole of the plane flat on your work bench, insert the blade, and clamp it down with the cap iron. If the edge of the blade just touches the

bench when the blade is seated, the adjustment will be correct. While adjustment of the blade involves trial and error, this method ensures that the edge of the blade is parallel to the sole. Rub a little candle wax on the sole of the plane, and you are ready to begin.

Planing should be done with the grain to avoid tearout. Look at the two surfaces of the board that are perpendicular to the one you intend to plane. Study the lines of the grain as they rise to the surface that you will be planing. In the ideal case you will want to plane in the direction of the points made by the surface and the grain lines. In reality the grain may point in different directions at various places along the board. Unless it is nearly vertical, steeply rising grain will give more trouble than slowly rising grain; so try planing with the steeply rising grain. If you get tearout, try the other direction. If you still have trouble, you may have to plane half the board in one direction and the other half of the board in the other direction.

The edge of the board along the grain is the easiest surface to plane. Beginners should master planing edges first. Push down on the front end of the plane as you begin to hold it against the board. Don't use any more pressure than necessary because you are really supposed to be pushing the plane along the length of the board. Push down a little extra on the rear of the plane as you finish. Don't worry about keeping the edge perpendicular to the faces, just concentrate on taking a smooth cut that produces a single thin shaving from one end of the board to the other. If your plane

7

skips, then check three things. Either the blade isn't sharp, the flat of the blade has a slight bevel at the edge, or the beveled side of the edge is rounded over. As you become proficient, angle the plane slightly so the blade shears the wood instead of cutting it straight on. If your plane is tuned and the blade sharp, the tool will actually sing as it produces the most wonderful thin and curly strips of wood. It is these moments that make woodworking with hand tools so delightful.

When it is important for an edge to be perpendicular to the faces, I use a simple jig. A piece of plywood clamped to the side of the plane can ride against one face, but about ½ inch of material below the sole is needed to bring the blade over the edge to be planed. I used a 9 inch by 3½ inch piece of ¾ inch plywood and glued on two 9 inch by 1¾ inch pieces of ¼ inch hardboard to make the device pictured in this article. Notch the hardboard where the plane blade protrudes. I hold the rear handle in one hand and the front of the jig in the other hand when planing.

The bench plane has no peer in preparing the edges of two boards to be joined into a wider board. Readers will see what I mean if they hand plane the edge of a board that has been run through a jointer. The rotating blades of the jointer leave little ripples that are evident when you try to plane a thin shaving. It will take a few passes before you can remove a thin shaving from one end of the board to the other. The ripples from a jointer will prevent two edges from seating together perfectly, and when the edges are joined, a glue line will be evident no matter how tightly you clamp the boards. Hand planed edges will seat perfectly and moderate clamping pressure will yield a glue line that is invisible.

It is not hard to use a bench plane to prepare the edges of two boards for joining. If you have a jointer, by all means use it initially. Then clamp the two boards face to face in your vice so the edges to be joined can be planed at the same time. The faces that are together should ultimately be on the same side of the glued up piece. Then it does not matter if the edges are not quite perpendicular to the faces, because the edges will complement each other when the two boards are joined. Plane the edges a little more in the center so they are slightly concave. This ensures that the end will be tight, and it is easy to clamp the boards together in the middle.

Bench planes can be used to surface any board, but as a practical matter most woodworkers either own a planer or buy their lumber surfaced on two faces. Such lumber can be joined to form wider boards without further work, but eventually the faces of all boards need further smoothing. Except for using a drum sander, hand planing is probably the fastest and easiest method for flattening and smoothing the faces of a board. Don't clamp the board as this may bend it, but place it on a flat workbench against stops. If necessary, clamp a ¼ inch board to your workbench to make a stop. Plane with the grain, beginning at one edge and moving systematically across the face. The blade should be on the lowest setting that will produce a shaving, and you should

2. The long grain edge of a board is easily planed with the device for ensuring a right angle. Grasp the device at the front to balance the outrigger screw of the clamp as this makes for steady planing.

3. When joining two boards to form a wider one, clamp them together in your vice and plane both edges at the same time. Any errors in the angle of the edges will cancel if two faces clamped together are on the same side of the board. Hand planed edges yield an invisible glue line.

4. Planing the face of the board should be done against bench stops to avoid bending the board. Adjust for a minimum shaving and angle the plane for a shearing action. Systematically work your way across the face, and enjoy the shavings as they flow through the throat of the plane.

5. End grain planes nicely, but you must clamp a scrap at the end of the cut to avoid break out. Curl your fingers over the sole and against the wood to guide the plane.

6. Block planes excel for small work and are conveniently held in one hand. Put your forefinger on the front knob when you need additional pressure. The block plane works well for camfering and rounding corners.

7. Block planes will level protruding end grain to the surface of a face.

convex edge on the blade will make it easier to join plane strokes together without showing a ridge from the edge of the blade. The blade must be razor sharp, and you may have to resharpen from time to time to avoid tear out. Specialty blades made of particularly hard steel will not have to be sharpened as often but are somewhat harder to sharpen in the first place. Some grain is just too tricky to be planed successfully. If this is the case, complete the work with a scraper.

angle the plane so the blade shears. Take pleasures in the filmy shavings as they emerge from your plane. The shavings don't fill the air and fly all over the shop, and they are easy to clean up. The plane sings at a pleasant level. Without a hearing protector and a mask, woodworking becomes more enjoyable. A slightly

End grain can be planed perfectly well with a bench plane. No matter what type of plane you use, clamp a scrap of wood to support the board at the far end of the cut to prevent break out. I grasp the rear handle and the metal at the front end of

9

8. *A finger plane is even more controllable than a block plane.*

9. *A Record No. 073 rabbet plane will clean the cheeks of the tenon and size it for a perfect fit. Be sure the blade will shave and the throat is a minimum.*

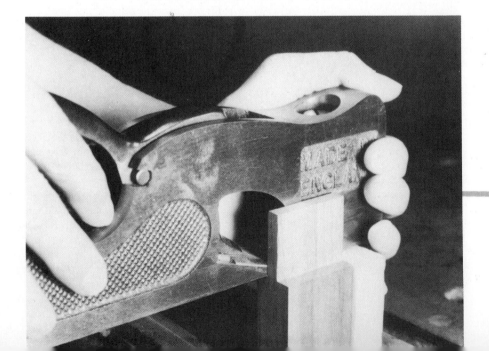

the plane so I can curl my fingers over the sole and against the wood. With this technique, I can use a fairly long plane on short boards, and the feel helps me keep the plane perpendicular to the faces.

Block planes are often used for planing end grain, but they are particularly convenient for planing with one hand. I use mine to round or camfer edges both with and across the grain. They are particularly handy for reducing the end of a through mortise and tenon to the level of the surrounding board. Make sure that the throat on your block plane is closed down to a minimum to prevent tear out. My finger plane is even easier to control than my block plane. I find the finger plane useful for planing down very small work, like protruding cross splines that I use to strengthen miter joints. Be sure to angle both these planes so the edge shears the wood.

My Record No. 073 rabbet plane is the secret to a tight fit in mortise and tenon joints. Again, it is imperative that the blade is sharp enough to shave, and the throat is adjusted to the minimum opening. Cut the mortise first, and then fit the tenon to the mortise using the No. 073. Clean up the cheeks of the tenon, checking the fit after removing each shaving. Take off just enough so that the tenon slides in snugly. Then smooth and adjust the shoulders of the tenon so they both butt tightly against the face with the mortise. Back up the shoulders with a scrap to avoid break out when planing across this end grain.

Try these hand planes. With a little practice you will no longer be satisfied with the results of using power tools alone.

10. *The rabbet plane is excellent for smoothing and adjusting the shoulders of a tenon so the joint seats tightly. You are planing end grain here, so be sure to back up your work with a scrap.*

About the Author:

W. Curtis Johnson is a contributing Editor to **The American Woodworker.**

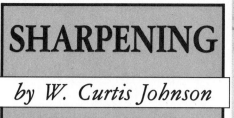

SHARPENING

by W. Curtis Johnson

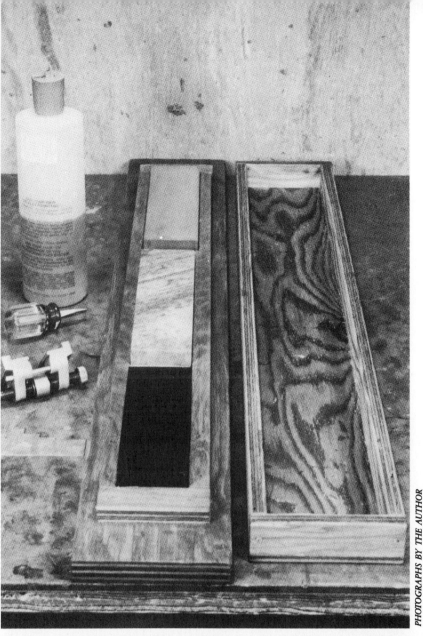

PHOTOGRAPHS BY THE AUTHOR

No cutting tool will perform well unless it is sharp. In the case of woodworking tools, this means they should be able to shave. Like skinning a cat, there is more than one way to do this. A glance through any woodworking catalog will reveal a bewildering number of systems for sharpening edged tools. I sharpen my plane blades and chisels on a set of bench stones, and they routinely give me an edge that will shave.

Having decided on the economical and reliable bench stones, there is still the choice between oil and water stones. Each has its advantages and disadvantages. Oil stones have been used by western woodworkers for years. The oil (I actually use kerosene) is used to float the small particles of metal and stone away. There are three basic kinds: silicon carbide (carborundum), aluminum oxide (india), and arkansas. Silicon carbide stones are artifically manufactured and cut relatively fast. They come in coarse through fine grits. These soft stones keep exposing new sharp particles and thus retain their cutting ability, but this same softness means they loose their flatness easily. Stones must be flat to sharpen plane blades, therefore woodworkers have tended to shun silicon carbide. Aluminum oxide stones are also manufactured but are much harder. These popular stones retain their flatness but cut slowly when the particles on the surface become dull. They also come in coarse through fine grits. Arkansas stones are found in natural deposits and are categorized into four hardnesses, all of which are relatively hard. The softest ''Washita'' stone is about the same as a fine silicon carbide or aluminum oxide. The other stones, in order of their hardness and fineness, are the soft arkansas, the hard arkansas, and the black hard arkansas. As you would expect, they retain their flatness well, but again the surface becomes dull with use.

A perfectly adequate set of oil stones for the woodworker would be a combination coarse-fine aluminum oxide stone and a hard arkansas. The coarse aluminum oxide would be used only for

My oil stones are always ready to sharpen a dull edge. A fine aluminum oxide stone, a soft arkansas, and a black hard arkansas are lined up in a holder that has a top to protect the stones from dust. Kerosene is conveniently stored in a shampoo bottle, and the honing guide with a screwdriver for tightening is close at hand.

grinding new bevels and grinding out nicks. The fine aluminum oxide would sharpen a dull edge while the hard arkansas would remove the burr created by the fine stone and hone the edge. A fancy set of oil stones might be a coarse-fine aluminum oxide combination, a soft arkansas, and a black arkansas. The soft arkansas would smooth the marks from the fine aluminum oxide so that the black hard arkansas could hone a particularly fine edge while removing the burr. The lore has it that one surface of each stone should be reserved for plane blades so it remains flat. In practice, I have never had a problem. If you use the entire surface of the stone when sharpening chisels and the like, it is not difficult to keep these hard stones flat across their width. Oil stones must be soaked in oil for a day when first purchased, but thereafter you need only put a little oil on the surface for each use.

Japanese water stones have recently gained popularity. These stones are usually manufactured but may be natural. They are soft and cut quickly, since new sharp particles are constantly being exposed. A typical set would be the 180 grit for shaping and removing nicks, the 1200 grit for sharpening, and the 6000 grit for polishing and removing any burr. They create a mirror finish that looks very satisfying, but the soft 6000 grit stone tends to round the edge slightly. These stones must be thoroughly soaked with water for any use.

I haven't been able to sense any difference in cutting ability between edges sharpened on the two systems, although the edge produced by the Japanese system certainly does look better. The advantages of oil stones are that they are hard and therefore retain their flatness, and they are always ready for use. The disadvantages of oil stones are that the oil will get on your work if you do not wash your hands and that dull surfaces must be renewed. The advantages of water stones are that the surfaces are always sharp and there is no oil to get on your work. The disadvantages are that concave surfaces must be renewed, they must be soaked in water to be ready for use, and sharpened edges that are not going to be used immediately must be oiled to avoid rust.

As far as I can see, both methods are equally messy. You either have oil in puddles or water in puddles, and the soaking of water stones seems to encourage larger puddles. Indeed, I find it more difficult to keep rust spots off my tools with the water stones than oil off my wood with oil stones. However, the new Japanese sharpening systems may eliminate this problem. Three stones are attached to a triangular block which sits over a plastic tub of water designed to submerge two stones when the third is being used.

You must renew the surfaces for both types of stones, either for flatness or sharpness. It is obvious when the Japanese stones are concave that something must be done. It is easy to flatten them with a sheet of 240 grit wet-and-dry silicon carbide paper glued to a flat surface. Use a little water as a lubricant and grind away. It is not so obvious that the surfaces of flat oil stones need to be renewed, but when they cut slowly, it's time to expose new, sharp particles. I use 400 grit silicon carbide in a water slurry between the surfaces of two stones as I rub them together. In the rare instance when the surface of an oil stone must be flattened, I use the silicon carbide slurry and rub the stone against a sheet of plate glass. Silicon carbide abrasive can be found at rock shops, auto body shops, and some art or hobby stores. Don't use a silicon carbide slurry with the Japanese water stones, since the carbide particles will embed themselves in the soft surface of the stone. Also, silicon carbide paper is not tough enough to completely renew the surface of a hard oil stone.

Which should you buy? That is hard to say, because on balance, I would judge that both systems are equally good (or bad). If you own a set of bench stones, I would just use those. A set of three Japanese stones is about the same price as the adequate set of oil stones described above, although the 6000 grit Japanese stone is finer than the hard arkansas.

Special guides can be fashioned, such as this one, for the small blade of a finger plane.

The Japanese system with the plastic water reservoir are about the same price as the fancy set of oil stones, which includes the extremely fine and expensive black hard arkansas. Either way, there is no free lunch. The important thing is to have a sharpening system that is ready to use so that you are encouraged to keep your tools sharp.

I bought a fancy set of oil stones a long time ago. I have them lined up, end to end, in a wooden box that is firmly fixed on my work bench so I'm always ready to sharpen a dull tool. A top keeps dust off of the stones. The kerosene is kept ready for use in a shampoo bottle with a squirt top. I prefer kerosene to oil because it is thin and lets the metal contact the stone for full cutting power.

Sharpening a chisel or plane blade begins with a 25° bevel. It is tempting to use a bench grinder to form this rough bevel or remove nicks, but I've never liked this process. It is just too easy to overheat the metal and ruin the tool completely by drawing its temper. If you must use a grinder, be sure that the wheel is dressed so that it cuts well. Wheels of granulated aluminum oxide, which resist glazing because the grains wear off easily, are now available from a number of mail order houses. In any case, use plenty of water and be very careful. A fine edge is more susceptible to overheating, so it's safer to save the final grinding for the coarse bench stone. For years, I did all my rough grinding on the coarse aluminum oxide bench stone, so it's possible. However, it's also a lot of work, and recently I bought a motorized stone that is water cooled which gives me the best of both worlds.

In every article I've ever read on sharpening, the author finds the bevel and then sharpens away on a bench stone while confidently maintaining a constant angle. I'll have to admit that I use a sharpening guide. That may be cheating, but I always get superb results. Construct a simple jig to measure the distance from the guide to the edge of the blade for obtaining 25, 30, and 35° angles. I scratch appropriate marks on the cap iron. Set the guide for 25° and form the first bevel.

I use a guide to maintain the proper angle when sharpening. Sharpen until you can just feel a burr at the flat side of the blade.

Remove the burr and hone the edge on your finest stone. Use two strokes on each side, alternating sides until the burr falls off.

New plane blades show deep marks from the tools which machined them. The flat part of the blade must be smoothed and have a polished surface from the finest sharpening stone at least 1/8 of an inch back from the edge.

The flat of a new plane blade can be smoothed on bench stones. Hold it flat and across the stone, pressing hard at the edge to grind imperceptibly more at this point. Although I prefer my oil stones for normal sharpening, I like the water stones better for this task.

Final sharpening should be at a 30° angle. I've tried 25° for the final angle and the metal just isn't strong enough to keep from chipping out. Indeed, I use 35° on chisels when I will be driving them with a mallet. A 25° bevel can be sharpened ten to twenty times at 30° before the 25° bevel must be renewed. I reform the edge at 25° when the 30° bevel occupies about one third of the total bevel.

The general procedure for final sharpening is easy. Begin on the fine aluminum oxide or medium grit water stone, and sharpen until you just feel a burr. Smooth the bevel with a few strokes on any intermediate stones. Use your finest stone to remove the burr and hone the edge. Simply alternate between the two sides of the edge giving two strokes each time. A total of twenty strokes, that is, five pairs of strokes on each side of the edge, should remove the burr and polish the bevel.

Final sharpening is slightly different just after the 25° bevel has been formed because the rough stone has already produced a large burr. Two or three strokes at 30° on the fine stone should be enough to produce the steeper bevel. Hone this bevel and remove the burr in the normal way. Each time you sharpen at 30° it will take another stroke or two because you must remove more metal as the bevel widens. When the number of strokes necessary to produce a burr becomes unreasonable, redo the 25° bevel.

One refinement in sharpening is to consider the width of the tool. You have to remove more metal from a plane blade than you do from a chisel to produce the same bevel. Thus, the pressure you put on the tool while sharpening should be commensurate with the amount of metal you want to remove.

So far I have only discussed smoothing one side of the edge, but clearly both sides must be equally smooth if the edge is to be sharp. Do not put a second bevel on the flat side of tools like a plane blade or a chisel, or they will not cut well. Instead, it is necessary to bring the flat side of the blade to the polish produced by your finest honing stone. You really don't have to do this for the entire surface of the blade, but the blade *must* be kept flat against the stone during the procedure. First renew any dull or cupped surfaces on the stones, as you will be removing a lot of metal, and all surfaces must be true. Choose a stone that will make somewhat finer scratches than the surface left by the manufacturer. This will probably be your standard sharpening stone. Place the blade flat and across the stone. The blade should be perpendicular to the stone, and across the full width of the stone with the edge close to one side. Press hard about ¼ of an inch back from the edge and move the blade along the length of the stone to grind the flat. Applying pressure near the edge will create a very long and imperceptible bevel that can be tolerated. Grind until you have produced a new smoother surface at least 1/8 of an inch back from the edge. Now, repeat with any intermediate stones and polish the flat with your honing stone. This surface should now see only a honing stone when you are sharpening.

It is easy to put off sharpening a tool when working on a project, but that is a mistake. You really need a sharp tool, and the task isn't difficult. The methods described here will give you a tool so sharp that it will shave, and the sharp tool is what you really need to get the project done quickly and easily. Take the time to do it right.

ABOUT THE AUTHOR:
W. Curtis Johnson is a contributing editor to The American Woodworker.

Tuning A Hand Plane

by W. Curtis Johnson

The common hand planes do not come ready to use as purchased. This may well be the reason these valuable tools have dropped from favor. The crudely made planes do not perform well, and the frustrated woodworker finds another way to smooth or trim the project. Yet the hand labor necessary to properly finish a plane is expensive and would price the product beyond the budget of most people. Having the purchaser finish the hand plane is a compromise, but a sensible one. No special tools are needed, and the woodworker can probably afford his own labor.

Turning a crude tool into a precision instrument is called tuning. While some may consider it annoying, tuning does create a personal relationship between the woodworker and his tool. The easiest way to save time in tuning is to select a well made tool to begin with. The quality from a single manufacturer varies tremendously. I mail ordered my jack plane and had to remove a ferocious amount of metal to flatten its concave bottom. The smoothing plane that I am tuning for this article was the best of five I found at a hardware store in Bristol, England. It's going to need very little work. I'm going to concentrate on bench planes because they are more complicated than most. Simpler planes merely have fewer parts to tune. Refer to the first article in this series for the names of the parts making up a plane.

The first consideration in selecting a metal bench plane is the frog. If this isn't machined correctly, it may be difficult to repair the errors. Remove the lever cap and lift out the cutting iron (blade) together with its cap iron. The frog is cast, so it's not going to look perfect, but the bed on which the blade rests should be flat; the frog should sit squarely on the bottom of the plane and the step that accepts the locking screws. This seat for the frog should be well cast. There is some play when the locking screws are loose, and

it should be possible to position the bed perpendicular to the sides of the plane. Bring a square and a screwdriver to the store or ask to borrow these items from a display.

Now check the bottom of the plane for flatness. This isn't too important for a short plane, but a slightly convex or concave bottom on a long plane can translate into a lot of metal that will have to be removed. Put a straight edge along the sole and hold it up to the light. A warp of 1/32 of an inch is not uncommon for longer planes, but you should be able to do better than that. The sole must be flat right up to the edges of the mouth, so beware of planes that are rounded at the opening. You will probably have to settle for something less than perfection. Check that the sides of the plane are perpendicular to the sole. This aspect should be pretty good as it would be difficult to correct.

It's nice if the mouth of the plane has parallel edges which are perpendicular to the sides of the plane, but this defect is relatively easy to correct. Check over all the other parts of the plane for obvious problems. Purchase the best plane you can and plan on tuning it.

Tuning begins with the mouth. Use a broad, fine file to make both edges of the opening perpendicular to the sides of the plane. Don't remove any more metal than you have to, and keep the angles the same as they were originally. Take your time and work carefully on this important step. If the opening on your plane is particularly skewed, use a square and scribe lines to define new edges for the mouth. Actually, the size of the opening is not too important if the frog on your plane is adjustable. I filed a larger mouth on my jack plane so that it could accommodate some of the thicker specialty blades.

True the sole next. The frog should be tightened in place since this can affect the shape of the bottom. If the mouth is adjustable, as with a block plane, make sure that this is tightened in approximately the correct spot. There are a number of ways to flatten the sole, and they all work. The simplest is to have your local machine

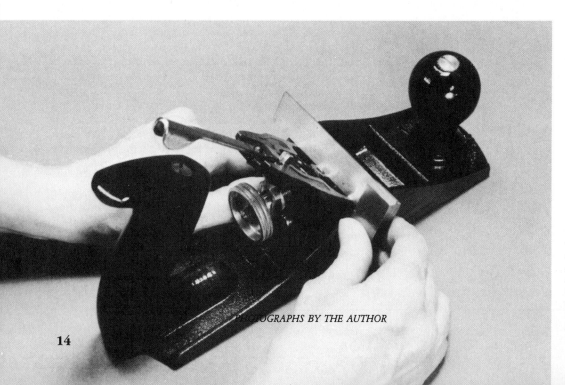

PHOTOGRAPHS BY THE AUTHOR

Be sure that the frog on the plane that you purchase has a flat bed which can be positioned perpendicular to the sides. A defect here is difficult to correct, since it requires filing the mating surfaces between the frog and the body of the plane.

14

Begin tuning a hand plane by carefully filing the mouth so it has parallel edges that are perpendicular to the sides of the plane. Keep the same angles that were manufactured into your tool.

"If your plane is far out of true ...take it to a machine shop"

As purchased, a plane will have a rough sole which is probably also out of true.

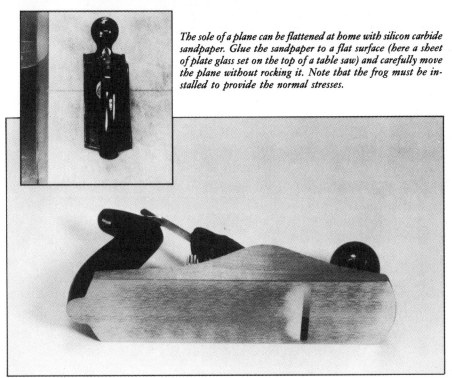

The sole of a plane can be flattened at home with silicon carbide sandpaper. Glue the sandpaper to a flat surface (here a sheet of plate glass set on the top of a table saw) and carefully move the plane without rocking it. Note that the frog must be installed to provide the normal stresses.

100 grit silicon carbide paper will true the sole of a plane with the high spots showing as the smoother patches. Check your work periodically with a straight edge to be sure that you are really improving the flatness of the sole. Further smooth the sole by progressing through the finer grits, stopping with 400.

shop true the bottom, but this will probably double the cost of your plane. If your plane is long and far out of true, I'd take it to a machine shop. After ten hours of work and ten dollars in materials, the cost will look pretty good.

My home method for truing a plane is to use silicon carbide paper glued to a perfectly flat surface. My flat surface is a piece of 3/16 inch plate glass clamped gently to the top of a table saw. I use spray adhesive to glue the paper to the glass. Glue several sheets in a row if you are truing a long plane. Silicon carbide paper is the black wet-and-dry sand paper and is commonly available in 240, 400, and 600 grits. A little water should be used to keep this paper from clogging. It is now available in a large range of grits as the white looking Fre-Cut paper manufactured by 3M. This silicon carbide paper is coated with zinc stearate which will keep it from loading up, and thus no water is needed.

Begin with 100 grit Fre-Cut paper. This is just like sanding a table top smooth, except that the paper is stationary and you are moving the plane. For a plane that is badly warped, you could begin with a belt sander using aluminum oxide grit to remove metal rapidly, but be very careful not to make the problem worse. I've seen various motions recommended for the hand sanding, but the only one that works

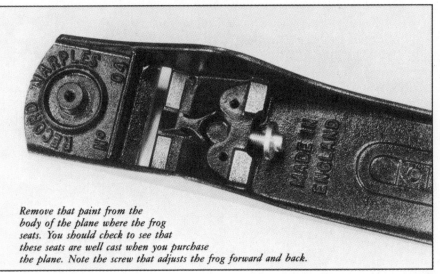

Remove that paint from the body of the plane where the frog seats. You should check to see that these seats are well cast when you purchase the plane. Note the screw that adjusts the frog forward and back.

The frog itself should have machined surfaces that fit tightly on the seat. This is another important point to check when purchasing a plane. The two screws that hold the frog in place are also shown here.

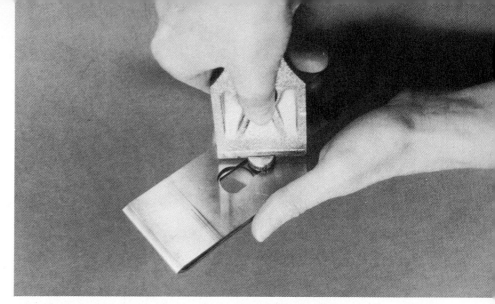

The lever cap should be trued at the end so it presses against the cap iron across its entire width. Here we see the blunt end of the cap lever used as a screwdriver to remove the cap iron from the cutting iron.

There is no point in polishing the sole as it will become scratched with use.

Position the frog so the blade is parallel to the front edge of the mouth forming a throat about 1/32 of an inch wide. This will work well for all but the roughest planing. Here we see the sole smoothed with 400 grit silicon carbide paper, a bright reflection from the sharpening bevel on the plane blade, and the throat as a 1/32 inch dark shadow.

for me is to cut on the push stroke as if planing a piece of wood. Lift the plane to return it to the front of the paper and make sure the plane remains perfectly flat on the paper as you push. More complicated motions tend to rock the plane making the bottom convex. As you check the bottom, the smoother patches from your sanding denote the high spots and will contrast with the original finish. Use a straight edge periodically to be sure that you are improving the flatness of the sole. If you are removing too much metal at the ends, try starting with the back off of the sandpaper and following through with the front of the paper. This will sand the center more. Also, holding the plane at the frog may help prevent rocking. Continue until the original finish is gone. The sole should now be truly flat, but it should be smoother for easy planing. Just progress through the grades as if you were sanding a piece of furniture. This should go fairly quickly. Stop at 400 grit. There is no point in polishing the sole as it will become scratched with use. The sole of the plane should now be smooth and true, and the front edge of the mouth should sport a sharp corner. The sharp corner is important to reduce tear-out when planing. The sharp angle on the rear edge of the mouth should be chamfered slightly with a file to avoid gouging when planing. Also chamfer the outside edges of the sole.

Now, remove the paint from the seat of the frog on the body of the plane. Install the frog and scrutinize it with the blade in place. Presumably you have already checked with a square to make sure that the bed of the frog is flat and can be adjusted perpendicular to the sides of the plane. Flatten a warped bed with a file. Correct an ill fitting frog by filing the mating

The cap iron should be sandwiched to the cutting iron so the edge of the chip breaker is about 1/32 of an inch from the sharpened edge of the blade. The polish on the chip breaker is evident here.

The chip breaking end of the cap iron should be squared to its sides and the chip breaking surface smoothed and polished. Then sharpen the end and smooth the inside edge so the chip breaker fits snugly against the plane blade with no gaps.

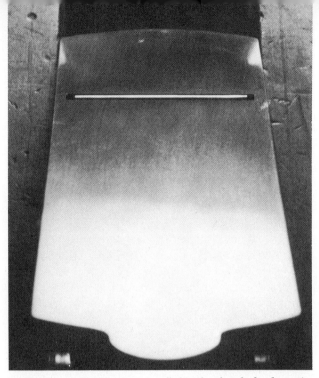

With the cap and cutting irons installed in the plane body, the cutting edge of the blade can be positioned so it is parallel to the sole. View the plane along the sole, and use the adjusting lever to even the dark shadow at the throat.

surfaces on the frog and the plane body. I'm going to discuss sharpening separately, but for this test, the cutting edge of the iron must be perpendicular to the sides of the blade. Use a file to do this; the blade need not be sharp. It should be possible to adjust the frog so the cutting edge of the blade is parallel to the sides of the mouth while it is at the same time adjusted parallel to the sole of the plane. If the plane fails this test, you will need to do more work. Fortunately, most high quality planes are made well enough to pass this test without any tuning. While you are at it, use the adjusting screw to position the frog so the cutting edge of the blade and the front edge of the mouth form a "throat" about 1/32 of an inch wide. If you take thick shavings, the throat will have to be wider, but I find 1/32 of an inch practical for all the planing I do.

On bench planes, file the cam on the lever cap so it works smoothly against the spring. The end of the lever cap should be trued so it presses against the cap iron across its entire width. Don't sharpen the end however, as the blunt end makes an excellent screwdriver to remove the cap iron from the cutting iron.

The chip breaking end of the cap iron should be square relative to the sides. Depending on the problem, you may have to bend or file it. It also must be sharp, smooth, and fit tightly against the cutting iron. Remove any nicks from the rounded top surface of the chip breaker with a fine stone and then polish it; the shavings will be sliding over this surface. On a new plane you will probably see gaps when you hold the sandwich of cap iron and cutting iron up to the light. Smooth and straighten the inside edge of the chip breaker by running its breadth along the length of a medium grit sharpening stone. Rest the top end of the cap iron against a board that is lower than the top of the stone to maintain the correct angle. For a standard 5 inch long cap iron, the top should be about ¾ inch lower than the chip breaker. With the proper bevel only the straight, sharp edge of the chip breaker will contact the blade. A tight fit prevents the

shavings from jamming between the chip breaker and the cutting iron.

Excessive play can be improved in most adjusting mechanisms, but you are not going to eliminate it completely. Indeed, after you have adjusted the blade, you will want to back off the pressure a bit so the blade doesn't slowly move forward. Don't tamper with older bench planes that have the adjusting fork cast as a single piece; you will just break the fork. Newer bench planes have a sheet metal fork made in two pieces. Bending one arm to offset it from the other will eliminate the play both at the depth-adjusting nut and the rectangular hole in the cap iron. Block planes with a vertical adjustment have the depth-adjusting nut riding inside a fork. Pinch the fork so it bears against the nut. Block planes with a horizontal adjustment have an adjuster with a hole that rides in a groove. Since the nut is permanently attached to the shaft, it is difficult to bend the adjuster to improve the play in this mechanism.

The smoothing plane tuned here is the first one I have bought where the handle is unsatisfactory. The edges are only partially rounded. If necessary, soak the handle in lacquer thinner to strip the finish and reform the handle to suit your grip. I would round the corners here. Thinned linseed oil is excellent for any wooden handle since it is less likely than glossy finishes to cause blisters.

Obviously it is still necessary to sharpen the blade, and this will be treated in the next article. With a sharpened blade, assemble the plane. Mount the cap iron on the sharp cutting iron and adjust the edge of the chip breaker back about 1/32 of an inch from the cutting edge. Seat this sandwich on the bed of the frog and tighten the cap lever screw until you are just able to snap the lever cap in place with the cam. Sighting along the sole of the plane, use the adjusting lever to position the cutting edge of the blade parallel to the sole. Rub a little candle wax (paraffin) on the newly trued sole. Now you have a precision instrument that will make beautiful shavings a few thousands of an inch thick with very little effort.

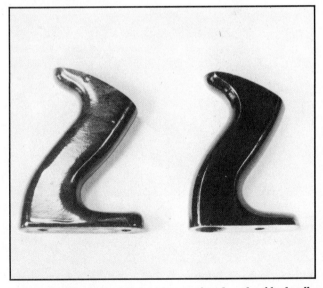

The new handle on the right has edges not found on the older handle. Strip the finish and shape the handle to suit your grip. Refinish the handle with thinned linseed oil.

ABOUT THE AUTHOR

W. Curtis Johnson is a contributing editor to **The American Woodworker.**

The Answer: Hand Planes

Editor's note: *The following discussion of hand planes is excerpted from "The Answer," a column by Ernie Conover that appeared regularly in* American Woodworker.

Q. Which type of hand plane is better, wood or metal?

A. I think this often-asked question stems from the feeling that the beautiful wood planes offered by most tool sellers must be better. I wish this were true, because I sure would like an excuse to buy one. But the truth of the matter is that wood and metal planes perform about the same.

Each type does have some advantages. Because of wood's low coefficient of friction, wood planes glide over the work with less effort. Aesthetically, they are pleasing to hold and own. In fact, I think this is the single most important factor that captivates most wood plane aficionados.

Metal planes are much easier for the average person to adjust. This alone makes metal planes a good starting tool. Learn to plane with metal, then move on to wood if you want to. Most good metal planes produced in the last 100 years have precise controls for adjusting the mouth opening and moving the iron both up and down and side to side. Rubbing a little candle wax on the sole once in a while will greatly reduce friction, making metal glide almost as well as wood.

Much more important than the material of manufacture is that a plane be properly tuned. No plane works well fresh out of the box; planes always benefit from a little doctoring. Make sure the sole is really flat, with no rounding around the mouth. If necessary, put a piece of emery cloth or sand paper on the bench and rub the plane body on it until flat.

Hone the iron with a series of wet or water stones until it is razor sharp. You may want to grind the edge slightly convex (up to 1/64 inch) and hold it to an angle of 30 degrees. Make sure that the cap iron fits well, with no gaps. It should be placed from 1/64 inch to 1/16 inch behind the edge, depending on the class of work. Finally, keep the adjustments modest. Most beginners try to take too heavy of a cut.

Q. I have several old planes with the term "cast steel" stamped in the iron. What is cast steel?

A. Cast steel is a process developed in the late eighteenth century in Sheffield, England. Up until the invention of this process, most cutting tools were made from carbonized steel. That is, a blank of steel was packed in charcoal and brought to a high temperature. This imparted enough carbon to the surface of the steel to heat-treat it for a working cutting edge. The problem was that the carbon content was not consistent throughout the entire cross-section of the tool. As a result, repeated sharpening would grind the tool down to its core, which would not hold an edge. To avoid this problem, edges often were created by "steeling." In this process, a piece of high quality steel was placed at the edge of a tool and attached by the act of hammer-welding in the forge. Thus, an expensive piece of steel was backed by a relatively cheap piece of steel.

The term "cast steel" signifies that the steel was made in a true steel-making process in a crucible and poured into an ingot. The ingot was then rolled out into bars for subsequent manufacture of tools. This term became quite widespread and cast steel tools were so much superior to older carbonized rod iron tools, that the stamp "cast steel" became a mark of excellence. Although it is mostly found on tools from the Sheffield, England, area, the term is also used elsewhere.

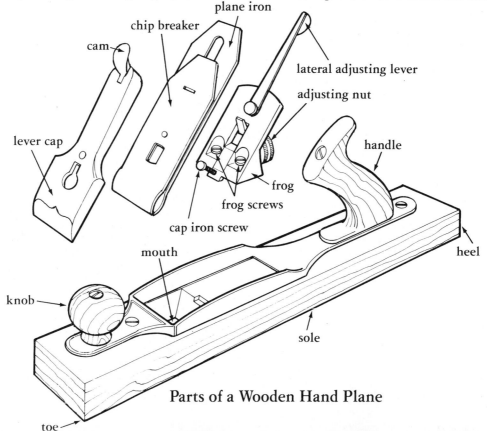

Parts of a Wooden Hand Plane

The Scraper

By W. Curtis Johnson

The scraper is just a rectangular piece of sheetmetal, but it is one of the most useful tools in a woodworker's shop.

The burr on the edge of a scraper will slice thin, clean shavings from a piece of wood. It can be used instead of a plane or sandpaper to smooth boards, remove glue, or clean up inside corners. Its cost is low, ranging from $2.50 for the generic model to $7.00 for the Sandvik scraper which is made of Swedish steel and comes presharpened in its plastic sheath.

In spite of its utility, the scraper is not a popular tool so you probably won't find it at your local hardware store. However, skiers now use them to smooth the bottoms of their skis and many sporting goods stores carry them. In any case, they are readily available from the mail order houses.

A scraper will last virtually forever, but it does have to be sharpened from time to time. This need not be difficult or

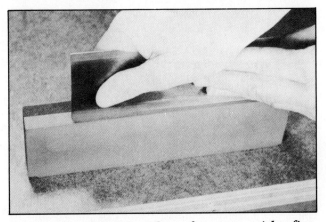

Fig. 3. *Smoothing the edges of a scraper with a fine sharpening stone.*

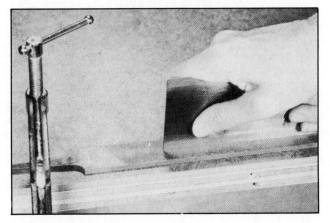

Fig. 2. *Removing the old burr and squaring the corners of a scraper with a mill file.*

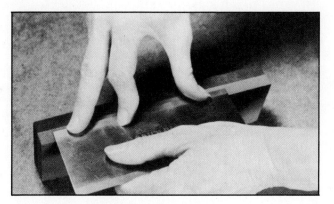

Fig. 4. *Smoothing the flat surface of a scraper with a fine sharpening stone.*

time consuming. The aim is to produce square, smooth corners that can be turned to give a sharp burr (called burnishing). As shown in Fig. 2, I square the corners and remove the old burr by clamping a large mill file to my workbench and running the scraper, which I hold vertically, against the teeth of the stationary file. Ten strokes on each edge should do the trick. The corner will now have a burr that you can feel with your thumb, but it is neither regular nor strong. I use the side of a fine sharpening stone to smooth the corner and remove this burr. Using the side of the stone prevents damage to its normal sharpening surface. Run the edge and the two flat surfaces along the stone to smooth the two corners (Figs. 3 and 4). Five strokes each, alternating among the three surfaces should be enough. Clean the grit off of the scraper.

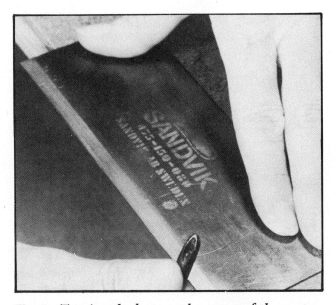

Fig. 5. Turning the burr on the corner of the scraper with a number 2 phillips screwdriver.

With the corners smooth and square you are ready to turn the burr on your scraper. There is no need to buy a special tool as any hard and smooth piece of metal will do. I prefer the round shank of my number 2 phillips screwdriver, but others prefer a flat tool such as a chisel. Apply a drop of oil to your burnisher for lubrication, and hold the scraper flat

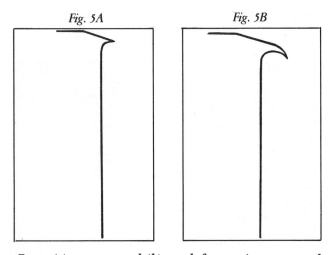

Burrs (a) correct, and (b) weak from using too much pressure.

with its edge extending over the side of your workbench as shown in Fig. 5. Tilt the burnisher about 10 degrees from vertical and gently but firmly run it along the top corner of the scraper. It does not take much pressure to turn the burr, and if the pressure is not sufficient you can always do it again. Test the corner with your thumb. You should feel a small burr. The idea here is to create burrs with a lot of strength,

Fig. 6. Sharp scraper cutting a curly shaving.

similar to the one illustrated in Fig. 5a. If you apply too much pressure the burr will roll over and be weak like the one illustrated in Fig. 5b. Turn burrs on the other three corners. No matter how well you have turned the burrs your scraper will still be useable, so don't make a fetish out of it.

"It does not take much pressure to turn the burr..."

Now you can try your scraper and evaluate the burrs by smoothing the surface of a board. Some woodworkers believe the scraper should be pushed while others believe it should be pulled. I find the quality of the cut to be independent of direction, although pushing is more comfortable for me. Bend the scraper slightly with the curve in the direction of cut to keep the corners from gouging. Tilt the scraper until the burr just catches. Tilting further will shorten the life of the burr. When the scraper is sharp it will cut curly shavings from a smooth board as shown in Fig. 6. If you are tilting the scraper about 20 degrees from vertical, you have turned a good strong burr. The further you have to tilt the scraper to get it to catch, the weaker your burr. Applying less pressure when you burnish will produce a stronger burr that requires less tilt.

Fig. 7. Flattening the burr in preparation for turning a new one.

Strong burrs will last for a long time, but when they become dull there is no need to go through the entire sharpening procedure again. Burrs can be flattened and reformed five to ten times before squaring and smoothing are necessary. Simply use your burnisher to turn down the burr (Fig. 7) by running it a few times along the flat of your scraper. Then burnish the scraper with the tool vertical before tilting it 10 degrees to turn the burr in the normal way.

You will find the scraper superior to sandpaper for many applications. It will cut faster than rough sandpaper and outlast many sheets before it needs to be resharpened. Furthermore, the surface will be extremely smooth, equivalent to at least 220 grit sandpaper. When removing finish, the scraper will replace sandpaper and will not load up as sandpaper does. The scraper also removes soft or dried glue conveniently.

The scraper complements the plane. When a plane tears tricky grain, the scraper will smooth the area successfully. It will also smooth the small ridges which sometimes remain after planing the surface of a board. I often use the scraper instead of my Record 073 plane to smooth tenons and remove the last few thousandths for a perfect fit (Fig. 8). The tool fits into many hard to reach places, smoothing the inside corners of carcases or the inside of a rabbet (Fig. 9). Once you own a scraper you will wonder how you got along without it.

Fig. 8. Smoothing and dimensioning a tenon for a perfect fit.

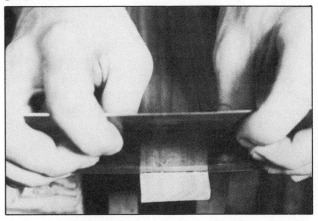

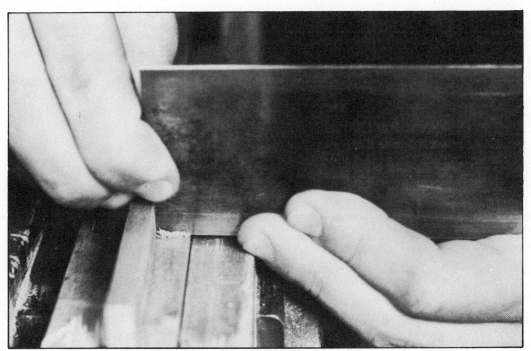

Fig. 9. Cleaning up a rabbet with a scraper.

Stationary Power Tools

SOME THOUGHTS FOR THE BEGINNER

By Dennis R. Watson

Before investing in stationary power tools you should have a thorough understanding of each tool's capability in relation to the type of work to be done. Some tools overlap in capability and you'll want to select the tool which satisfies your main objective, yet provides additional options as well. This added capability could eliminate the purchase of an additional tool. One of the first questions one needs to answer is: Do I really need a stationary power tool or will a portable power tool or a hand tool satisfy the requirement? Once you have determined a stationary power tool is needed, the second question becomes: What size and quality of tool do I need?

THE TABLE SAW, *depending on the type of work you are doing, could be your first investment in stationary power tools. The one shown above is a tilt table design, about 30 years old, and cuts extremely accurately. For fine furniture or cabinet work, a good table saw is a must.*

Generally, woodworking tools can be divided into two categories: industrial and home workshop. An industrial tool is designed and built to do precision work 24 hours a day, seven days a week with minimum maintenance. However, industrial tools are considerably more expensive than home workshop tools. A large selection of home workshop tools is available, ranging in quality that borders on inferior to excellence, and capable of accurate, dependable work. If you are doing fine cabinet or furniture work where precision is required, an investment in industrial machines could pay off. In any case, you'll want to buy the best tools you can afford, but if you are doing general woodworking or repairs around the house where great accuracy is not required, then a medium quality home workshop tool should work fine.

Most people would certainly think of a stationary circular saw as the first tool to buy. There are two general types of circular saws; the table saw and the radial arm saw. The table saw has the arbor/blade fixed and the wood is pushed past the blade to crosscut and rip. The radial arm saw is an altogether different concept in which the motor/arbor/blade moves along the arm to crosscut. To rip, the motor/arbor/blade is rotated and locked in position on the arm and the wood is pushed into the blade.

The table saw and the radial arm saw will both crosscut, rip, cut joints, etc., but each tool offers advantages over the other. The avid woodworker with a well equipped shop is likely to have both; a luxury most of us can't afford.

TABLE SAW - The table saw is the oldest of the two concepts and the first ones were designed with a fixed blade/arbor and tilt table, but as the use of 4 x 8 sheets of plywood became popular, the need for a stationary table with a tilt arbor/blade became desirable. However, in Europe where large sheets of plywood are not as plentiful, the tilt table version is still popular. Setting up the table saw for precision cutting is quick and once properly aligned the saw will maintain the setting for quite some time provided the operator is careful and does not abuse the machine.

The table saw excels in ripping; not only is it easier to rip on, but also, it's safer. For example, if the board becomes twisted or hung up, it's still free to pop up clear of the blade and fence; hence, kickback is minimized. Clearly the table saw excels for ripping, but I also prefer it for cutting joints and crosscutting small pieces of wood. In addition to the basic sawing operation, a moulding head can be used for cutting moulding or decorative edges and a sanding disk can be installed. The real disadvantage of the table saw is that space is required on all four sides. If you are a serious woodworker, interested in making fine quality furniture or cabinets, then by all means invest in the best table saw you can find and afford.

RADIAL ARM SAW - The radial arm saw excels in crosscutting, especially long boards which are otherwise awkward to cut on the table saw. Since the blade is above the wood, it is easy to align to the exact cutoff mark. Ripping with

If general repair or construction work is your forte, along with some fine furniture or cabinet work, then a good radial arm saw should work out fine.

JOINTER - Most people are familiar with the use of the jointer to remove saw marks and square the edge of a board to produce a gluing or finished edge; however, the jointer performs two other very important functions. A board which is irregular in width or simply bowed can be straightened with repeated passes over the jointer. When using the jointer to straighten a board, the width of the cutter is not as important as the length of the bed. The longer the bed, the easier it is to true the edge.

The other main function of the jointer is to remove cup from the surface of a board before it is planed to the desired thickness. To obtain a flat board after it has been thickness planed, it is necessary to have one flat surface to ride against the bed rollers or table of the thickness planer. Both cutter width and bed length are important.

Some jointers are designed with a rabbeting shelf which allows rabbets to be cut along the length of a board. The fence is slid to the left hand side and adjusted for the width of the rabbet. The depth of cut is controlled by lowering the infeed table and varies on most home workshop jointers from 1/8 to 3/8 inch. However, I have found running a rabbet is easier and more accurately done on the table saw or shaper.

Some tool manufacturers refer to the jointer as a jointer-planer indicating the jointer can be used to plane wood to a desired thickness. This is somewhat misleading, as a special jig or fixture (either homemade or purchased) is required. Surfacing wood to a desired thickness on the jointer is time consuming and requires cutting a rabbet on both edges of the board and set up time for the jig. Planing to a desired thickness on the jointer is possible, but it is best left to the thickness planer, a tool designed for the job.

the radial arm saw, however, is tense and nerve racking at best. Kickback is the most serious drawback; the board is confined in all four directions and if it becomes twisted or caught by the blade it has only one way to go — back toward the operator. The radial arm saw can be adjusted to cut accurately, but I have found the accuracy is difficult to maintain and constant checking is necessary. This is probably due to the complexity required to allow the head to swivel, tilt, and slide along the arm. In addition to the complex design, the head/blade is heavy and when crosscutting, this heavy mass is pushed back until it hits a rubber stop, which eventually results in a slight misalignment.

The radial arm saw has several advantages over the table saw; it is designed to be placed up against a wall with space only needed at the ends. In addition, most designs have a power take off on the right hand side of the motor which will accept a drill chuck, disk and drum sander. The drill chuck can turn the radial arm saw into an overhead pin router, horizontal boring machine and slot mortiser. Like the table saw, a moulding head can be used.

For fine furniture or cabinet work, the JOINTER is a must to straighten and square the edge of a board, and to remove cup from the surface of a board in preparation for the thickness planer. A homemade extension was added to the outfeed table.

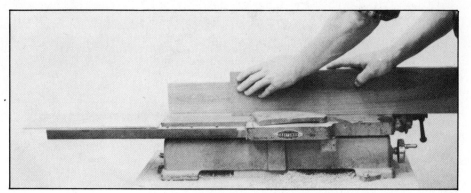

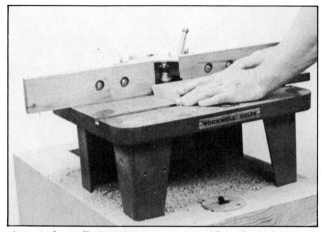

A vertical spindle SHAPER is a very versatile tool which can not only cut decorative edges and moulding, but can also cut dados, rabbets, and matched joints as seen in fine cabinets and furniture.

If the bandsaw is used primarily for cutting irregular shapes, rough out work for the lathe or other work where accuracy is not critical, then a high quality tool is not needed. However, if the bandsaw is being used for accurate resawing, cutting, joints or fine delicate work, then a high quality tool may be required.

Size of the bandsaw is determined by the distance between the throat and the blade, with 12, 14, 16, and 20 inch being standard sizes. The maximum depth of cut, which is important in resawing, is determined by the height above the table the upper guide can be raised. The bandsaw is a good addition to the shop, and you'll find yourself using it more and more.

LATHE - The lathe is a unique tool; it is the only tool required to turn a rough block of wood into a finished useful product. Basically two types of work are done on the lathe: between centers or spindle turning and face plate turning.

A good jointer is a must for any type of fine furniture or cabinet work. The size you select depends on whether you will be using it for an edge jointing or for preparation to the thickness planer.

SHAPER - Not only can a vertical spindle shaper be used to cut moulding and shape the edge of a board, but it also cuts rabbets, grooves, tongue and groove joints, etc. With a matched male and female cutter, decorative joints, as seen on fine cabinets and furniture, can be cut. A large selection of standard three wing cutters is available, either high speed steel or carbide tipped. In addition to stock three wing cutters, a shaper collar is available in which knives ground to your specifications can be used.

Many people will ask: why buy a shaper when a portable router or moulding head on a table saw will do the same job? A shaper is more versatile than either a router or a moulding head; there exists a greater selection of stock cutters and an infinite variety if you grind your own. The use of matched cutters such as the tongue and groove, glue line and decorative joint is possible. Also, I prefer the shaper over the table saw or radial arm saw for running rabbets or grooves because it's much easier and faster. If you want a ¼ inch groove run in a stile for a door panel, you simply use a ¼ inch straight cutter and adjust the fence for the depth of cut.

BANDSAW - The bandsaw is one of the most versatile and useful tools in the workshop. Of course, it excels in cutting irregular shapes, but it can also crosscut, rip and cut joints. It's the best tool for resawing: cutting a thick board, say two inches, into two one-inch boards.

The BANDSAW, of course, excels in cutting irregular shapes, but it can also crosscut, rip and cut joints. The bandsaw can become one of the most used tools in your shop.

The LATHE is a most unique tool in that it's the only tool required to complete a project. Lathe work is divided into two categories: between centers and face plate turning.

The size of the lathe is determined by the diameter of wood which can be turned between centers. To increase the diameter, some designs, known as gap bed lathes, have smaller ways or beds at the headstock.

In roughing out stock from square to round, a great deal of vibration can occur. To dampen the vibration, it's important for the lathe to be as heavy as possible and bolted to a heavy sturdy base. It's very difficult to substitute another tool for the lathe. Either you need a lathe or you don't.

THICKNESS PLANER - This is probably the biggest, most expensive tool you can select for the shop, and unless you are really into serious woodworking, you'll find it advantageous to buy your wood already surfaced. However, if you decide to buy a planer, there are a couple which are well suited for the home workshop and vary in size from 7 inches to 15 inches. Anything bigger than 15 inches and you're into a very expensive industrial machine. When selecting a planer, go all out and get one with both power infeed and outfeed.

I hope this article has provided some insight on the function of each of the tools and the order in which you may want to purchase them. Good stationary power tools are not only a pleasure to own and use, but they take a lot of the preparation work out of woodworking and free the craftsman to do fine detail and delicate work, which can only be done with skill and good handtools.

A small home workshop THICKNESS PLANER should be adequate for most home workshops. The one shown can surface boards up to 7¼ inches wide and has power infeed and outfeed.

The Answer: Stationary Power Tools

Editor's note: *The following discussion of stationary power tools is from "The Answer," a column by Ernie Conover that appeared regularly in* American Woodworker.

In our previous columns we have discussed the purchase of most of the major machinery needed in a small, self-sufficient shop. This month we will clean up the series with some of the smaller, and in some cases, "nice to have" machinery.

BAND SAW

A band saw is definitely one of the most useful pieces of machinery in the shop. I have two that I use for everything from cutting firewood (much quieter than a chain saw) to blanking out bowls for turning to roughing dovetails. In principle, the band saw is a simple tool, but to work well, it must be well made. Because it is a popular tool, there are a good many in the marketplace at a variety of prices and quality. Band saws have a greater range in quality than just about any other tool.

The most popular size for a band saw is 14 inches, probably because this is the size of the ubiquitous Delta design. In fact, I think that at the word "band saw" most people mentally see this machine. It has a table about 14 inches square and 42 inches high. The blade runs on two wheels yielding a 14-inch throat (the distance from the blade to the frame) and a 6-inch depth of cut. It has a cast iron frame and is

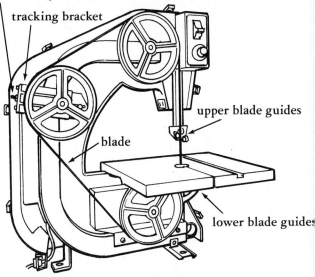

Parts of a Three-Wheel Band Saw

mounted on a stamped steel stand of varying degrees of enclosure and is powered, on average, by a ¾ horsepower motor.

Sound familiar? Well, it is a good, time-honored design that has been the basis of many other fine machines, and that has been slavishly copied in the Orient. If this is the type of machine you covet, then look at the Delta first, before any copycat machines. The copycats can be a very good buy, but as stated above, quality varies greatly. The important thing is to ensure that the seller will be there next year and is not operating out of the back of a rented 5-ton truck.

Recent years have seen a number of saws using three wheels. The main advantage of this type of design is that a much greater throat can be obtained in proportion to the frame and wheel size. The disadvantage is that the blade flexes more and blade life can suffer. But, with modern metallurgy, blades run longer than ever; so, life doesn't suffer much if the saw is reasonably well-built. High quality blades are, of course, more important than ever and will give true value for money spent.

The basic building blocks of any band saw are the frame, the wheels, and the guides. So, the buyer should focus his attention on these. The traditional material for frames is time-proven cast iron. But the casting on some of the recent copycat machines is pretty abysmal, so don't let the words "cast iron" charm you without some inspection.

In the last ten years, welded (or fabricated) steel and cast aluminum frames have come into use. Fabricated frames can be excellent; just check on the rigidity. Cast aluminum ranges from really bad, such as Sears, to excellent, such as Inca.

Wheels are made from cast iron, cast aluminum and die-cast alloy. All produce quite serviceable wheels, and the things to look for are strength and trueness. The wheel should be round and not run out when spun by hand. Any saw of reasonable quality today uses ball bearings in the hubs.

Guides serve the purpose of holding the blade straight and true on either side of the cut. The bottom guide is located below the table and is fixed. The top guide usually moves up and down on a rod so that it can be kept in proximity to the material being cut. A blade guard is usually attached to the

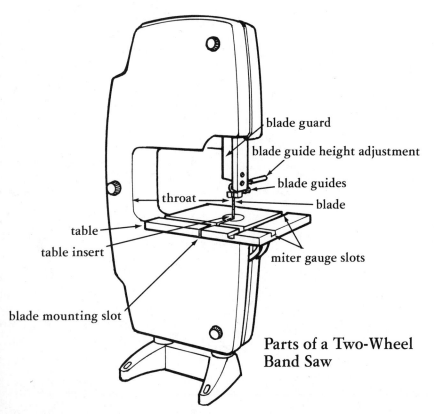

Parts of a Two-Wheel Band Saw

A Technique for Folding Band Saw Blades

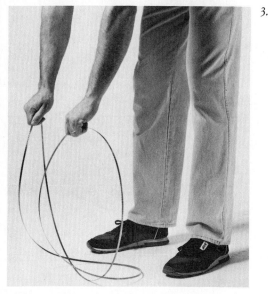

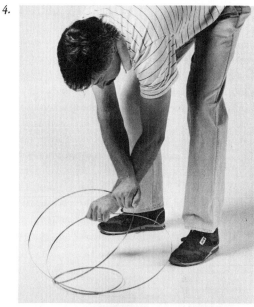

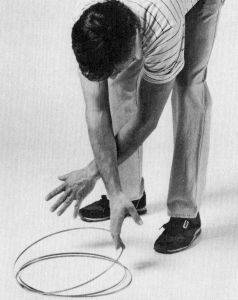

The safest way to fold a band saw blade is by lowering it to the ground as you fold it. **1.** *Begin by standing, holding the blade upright in front of you with the teeth facing away from you. Your hands should be slightly below the middle of the blade, with your thumbs up and your wrists flexed so your knuckles are turned in. The flat of the blade should be pinched between thumbs and index fingers.* **2.** *Now fold the blade forward by turning your hands down into the position you would use to push a wheelbarrow.* **3.** *Begin lowering the blade to the floor, moving your wrists closer together and twisting both wrists inward as you do so. The left wrist should twist in farther than the right.* **4.** *Continuing to lower the blade to the floor, pass your right arm over your left, causing the right loop of the blade to pass over the left loop.* **5.** *Lower the blade all the way to the floor, now folded into four loops. Release your left hand and then your right, dropping the folded blade onto the floor.*

same arm. The main things to look for in guides are that they indeed guide the blade and that they are easy to adjust. Cheaper guides use ball bearings to support the back of the blade, and fiber or wood block to support the sides. Better guides use ball bearings all around. Fiber guides have the advantage of being unable to harm the blade if they go out of adjustment. The best adjustment system is the micrometer type.

Finally, I would like to mention the several Japanese saws that have come on the market in the last five years. Strange looking things, they have tables that are low by western standards, and have really healthy throats and depths of cut. Although they are usually purveyed as band saws, they are actually resaws. They were designed for the purpose of resawing lumber (sawing large timbers into planks), and only secondarily as band saws. Surprise, surprise, the table height, throat size, and depth of cut turn out to be perfect for resawing tasks. But their high speed (usually 5,000 feet per minute) and guidance system designed for wide blades can make them a bit dangerous when used as a band saw. Even when refitted with after-market guides, blades of less than ⅜-inch width should not be run on these saws, or run only with extreme caution. Older models without rubber tires should not be used for narrow blades under any circumstances.

DRILL PRESS

Although you can get along without one, a drill press is certainly a useful tool. Taiwan now dominates this market, with Mainland China starting to enter the scene. Most of the old-line domestic manufacturers now confine themselves to the industrial "high end" market. Since a drill press is a simple, easy-to-build tool, a Taiwanese press can be a good value for the money. They build them along traditional lines, with plenty of metal and no frills.

Drill press features to examine are the capacity (the distance from the chuck center to the column), the size of the motor, the number of speeds, the length of stroke of the quill (the tube which houses the bearings and the spindle), the type of table, and how the table is raised and lowered. Capacity, power, and speeds are self-explanatory, but quill stroke should be a minimum of 4 inches for wood. A table which is raised and lowered via a rack and pinion mechanism is nice to have, as is angle adjustment. A production table (one with a well at the edge to catch coolant used in metalworking) is unnecessary for wood.

One thing worth mentioning here is hollow mortising chisels. This is an accessory that literally allows you to drill a square hole, and the applications for mortises are obvious. Very few Taiwanese presses can be retrofitted with hollow chisels; so, if you want to use them, check before you buy.

LATHE

Since our company manufactures lathes, I am a bit biased; a Conover Lathe is the best. Now that I have that off my chest, let's look at features. Capacity is the size of work that can be swung over the bed, and this is twice the center height. A lot of lathes have a gap in the bed so that a bigger piece can be swung on a face plate (such as a bowl) than between centers. Another factor to look at in swing is the height of the tool rest support. The real capacity is the size of piece that can be turned between centers over the tool rest support, and this is usually a minimum of 2½ inches less than the stated capacity.

Most lathes have unlimited swing by turning outboard off the back of the spindle. Many buyers spend a lot of time

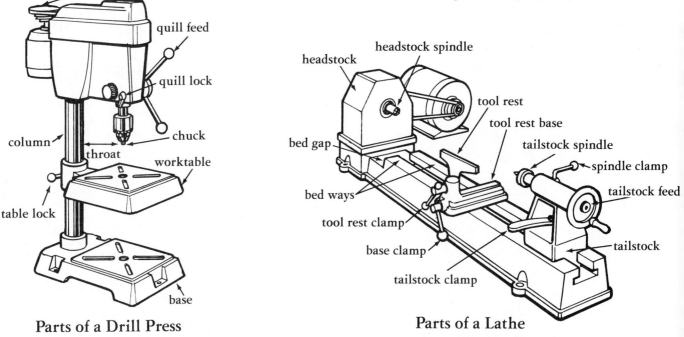

Parts of a Drill Press   **Parts of a Lathe**

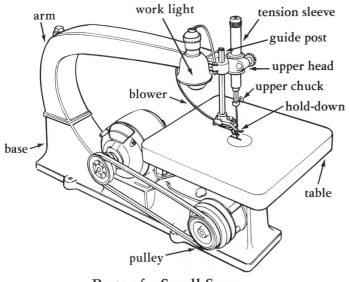

arm

work light

tension sleeve

guide post

upper head

blower

upper chuck

hold-down

base

table

pulley

Parts of a Scroll Saw

Always adjust the top guide of the band saw close to the stock to prevent the blade from bending and wandering. This is especially important when making curved cuts.

The mortising chisel allows you to use the drill press to make a clean, square mortise quickly and easily. The bit in the center of the tool excavates the bulk of the waste from the mortise, while the cutting edges of the housing around the bit square the mortise faces. This photo was set up to clarify how the tool works; when cutting an actual mortise, the working end of the tool is hidden from view.

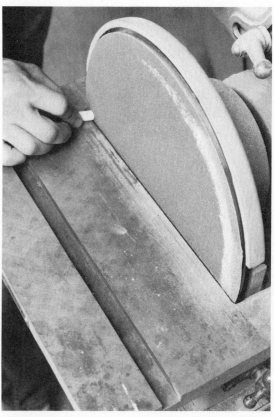

An easy way to check if your sander's disk is true is to rest a piece of chalk on the sander table and slowly bring it just into contact with the disk as it spins. If the disk is running true, you will get a continuous mark. If it is wobbling even the slightest bit, the mark will be broken.

worrying about outboard ability and end up turning one thing outboard in their entire lifetime. Most tail stocks today have a spindle travel which is too short. A minimum of 2½ inches of travel is necessary, and 4 to 5 inches is nice to have. The tool rest should be easy to move but rigid once set. Many tool rests have knobs that are in the way during high-angle cutting techniques.

A bench-top lathe can be a good buy, because one usually pays a lot for a sheet metal base. The two best bed materials are cast iron and wood, because they absorb vibration. A lot of lathes with fabricated steel beds are available today; these are to be avoided. This is one place in machine design where fabrication is just not as good as the time-honored methods. Steel transmits vibration and does nothing to dampen it.

Smaller lathes will run well with ½-horsepower engines, while most require ¾ or 1 horsepower. Big lathes use anywhere from 1½ to 3 horsepower, especially older machines with babbitt or brass bearings. The serious turner needs a good range of speeds. Many lathes today have rather high top speeds, but don't go slowly enough for large work. For large bowl work, a low speed of about 350 rotations per minute is needed, but a speed higher than about 2,500 rpm is just not necessary. Look carefully at how speed change is accomplished. The most convenient method is variable speed. If speed is changed by changing belts, make sure they come off quickly and easily.

Finally, look at the accessories available for the machine. Turning is a gadget business, and a machine that does not accept any of the exciting appliances available today is not worth owning.

One more point: Almost any machine can benefit by weighting it with sand. This can be done either by filling the base or by setting sand bags in place.

SCROLL SAW

The traditional name for this tool is a jigsaw, probably because the old Delta company marketed their machine under this name. The more modern nomenclature is scroll saw, and this actually may be the original term. It is interesting to note that the jigsaw is based on a hand-powered machine called a scroll saw. Patented in 1923, it is credited by many with starting the jigsaw puzzle craze of the Depression years. Many earned extra money by cranking out puzzles in their spare time. During those years, thousands of puzzles were made in the basements of America.

Jigsaw, scroll saw, who cares? They are both good descriptive titles.

For the life of me, I can't figure out where all the scroll saws on the market today are sold. There must be a volcano somewhere into which a government agency is pouring them. I don't see them as all that useful; they are rather a special purpose machine. Most woodworkers can do everything they need to do with a band saw and a hand jigsaw (or sabersaw). One only needs a stationary jigsaw if he is doing puzzles, marquetry, instrument roses, or the like.

The main things to look for in a scroll saw are capacity,

construction, and features. Since most scroll work is on thin stock, any of the machines have enough depth of cut. The distance from the blade to the frame is the capacity that should be checked carefully. The length of the stroke would be another important consideration, as it dictates how fast cutting takes place and, to some extent, blade wear. Variable speed is a very nice feature because it allows great flexibility in cutting. Other nice-to-have features are a dust blower and a light; however both can be rigged up by the owner.

Jigsaws require very little power, and I have not really seen an under-powered one. Most machines use cast construction, and there are some good cast aluminum ones. Budget machines often use stamped steel extensively. A final consideration is that a jigsaw tends to be a very safe machine and an excellent starting point for young, aspiring woodworkers.

BELT AND DISC SANDERS

These very useful machines can be purchased separately or as a combination machine. A disc sander is not very handy for finish sanding because it is very seldom that sanding marks can be kept parallel to grain. A disc sander is great for sanding end grain and complicated angles and miters. This is why pattern makers favor disc sanders.

Disc sanders range in size from 10 inches to the 18-inch to 20-inch range. The main thing to look for is trueness of the disc and the table. An easy way to check the disc is to touch a piece of chalk to it while it is running. If the chalk marks all the way around, then the disc is true. Make sure the disc is clean so glue and sandpaper don't interfere with the mark.

The table should be large, rigid, and slotted for a miter gauge. The best table material is cast iron. Look closely at how the table is adjusted. Pattern makers' large disc sanders have micrometer adjustment, while average machines have scales and stops at the principle angles. A disc sander doesn't need much power.

A belt sander is mostly a finishing tool because sanding can be kept parallel to the grain, but it does not hold exact angles well. The most popular size is a machine running 6-by-48-inch belts, although belts come in a variety of sizes. A machine running the 6-by-48-inch belt is a good home workshop choice because these belts are inexpensive and readily available.

Things to check on any belt sander are the platen, the rollers, the tracking mechanism, and the table. The platen is the plate in back of the belt but between the rollers. On better machines it is adjustable. On a new machine the crown in the rollers should be about 1/16 inch higher than the platen. The platen can be cast iron or stamped steel. The rollers should be true and run in ball bearings. The tracking mechanism is most important. A micrometer adjustment at both sides of the belt is best, but only available on top-of-the-line machines. Make sure a system is quick and easy to use, because it is something you will do frequently. The same criteria for the disc table apply to a belt table.

The Answer: Table Saws

Editor's note: *The following discussion of table saws is from "The Answer," a column by Ernie Conover that appeared regularly in* American Woodworker.

Personally, I'd rather have a table saw than a radial arm saw for serious cabinetmaking. The radial arm saw certainly has its place and accomplishes repetitive crosscuts more quickly and accurately. But when it comes to cabinetmaking, the table saw has the edge.

In concept, the table saw is a simple device. It's a circular blade spinning on an arbor and projecting through a slot in a table. While the Shakers often are credited with inventing the table saw, this tool actually was developed long before that time. Over the years, manufacturers have come up with many variations. In today's market there are a great many machines available, ranging in price from about $150 to $5,000. Obviously, some background information is necessary to make an intelligent buy.

SAW CAPACITY

The first thing a salesman will want to discuss is the capacity you want in a saw. Saw capacity is rated by the size of the blade, being 8, 9, 10, and 12 inches respectively, for most home workshops and light industrial machines. The fact is that the size of the blade doesn't always mean a lot. More important is the actual cutting capacity of the machine and the size of the table. It is possible for some 9-inch machines to outperform some 10-inch machines under these criteria. As a rule of thumb, it is important that the saw be able to cut through 2-inch stock at either 90 or 45 degrees of blade tilt and that a 12-inch-wide board be able to be rested squarely on the table in front of the blade. But the size of the table you need depends largely on the type of work you will be doing. Obviously, if you're a model maker, table size is relatively unimportant. However, if you are going to be doing a fair amount of work with plywood, it is nice to have good support for a 4-by-8-foot sheet when you rip it in half.

MATERIALS

Table saw tables traditionally have been made of cast iron. Today, however, other materials often are used. At lease one manufacturer now is using a plastic compound that looks very much like cast iron and has some interesting features. Only time will tell what its service life will be. Other "modern" materials are cast aluminum and stamped steel. Cast aluminum can make a very serviceable table, especially if hard-coat anodized. Stamped steel, on the other hand, has some real disadvantages. Very rarely is it truly flat, and it is prone to warping. Stamped steel tables should be avoided if possible. Of course, flatness is an important feature in a table and should be looked at carefully. Don't get too hung up on flatness, though, because remember, we're cutting wood, not parts for the space shuttle. Suffice it to say that no table should have more than about $1/32$-inch run-out in any direction over its surface. The easiest way to check this is with a large straightedge, but be sure that the straightedge is ground and actually straight. A stamped carpenter's square isn't good enough. Simply hold the straightedge on the table and look for light under it. Also feel if it rocks. Forget about dial indicators for this purpose, as that kind of accuracy isn't needed.

EXTENSIONS

You can extend the table on most table saws by adding extension wings. These wings come in a variety of shapes and materials. When it comes to wings, some sacrifice in material and quality is acceptable, because they are only used to support work riding outboard, and flatness is not quite so important. For cutting plywood, stamped steel wings can be quite adequate. In the past, many saws were made with cast wings of an open grate type. This was done to save material in manufacturing. The trouble with open grate wings is that fingers can be pinched badly or even removed during kickbacks by being caught in the grating. I would not absolutely discard an open grating saw on the used market because of this, but be aware of the hazard. One quick cure is to fill the grate with a plastic compound such as that used on redwood burl tables.

MITER GAUGES

On a table saw, most crosscuts are done with the miter gauge, which fits into a slot or T-slot in the table. I wouldn't worry much about the quality of the mitre gauge. I have seen few, even on very expensive saws, that were really accurate, and these had to be set with a square anyway. T-slots are nice because the gauge can overhang the front of the table without falling on the floor. Again, when it comes to capacity it is nice to be able to put a 12-inch board in front of the blade with most of the miter gauge resting on the table.

Because miter gauges are never very accurate, the accuracy of any table saw can be greatly improved by building a jig. This type of a jig is best built from cabinet-grade, medium-density fiber board. Simply attach strips of wood, which are milled to the table slots, to the bottom of the piece of fiber board and bolt a stout piece of wood at either end to hold the

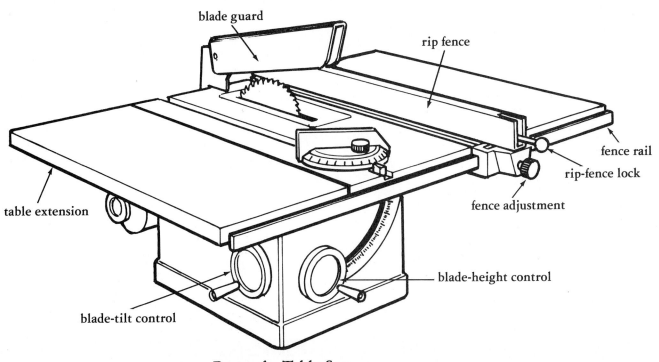

blade guard

rip fence

table extension

fence rail

rip-fence lock

fence adjustment

blade-height control

blade-tilt control

Parts of a Table Saw

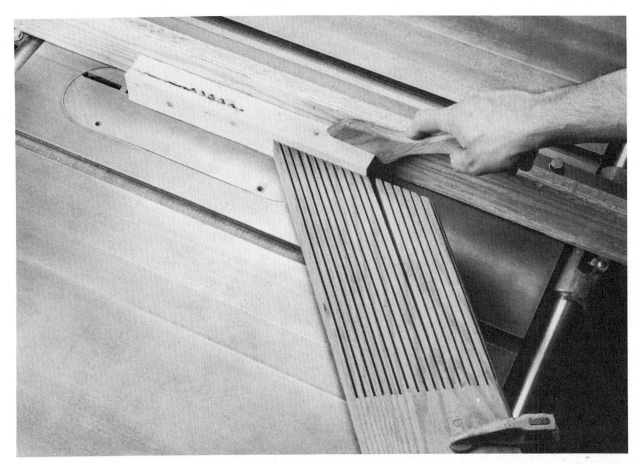

The push stick and the fingerboard are two accessories for the table saw that can easily be made in the shop. The fingerboard has a series of kerfs ripped into its mitered end, creating flexible fingers. When properly aligned and clamped to the saw table, it will allow stock to be pushed toward the blade, but will prevent it from being kicked back. In the bargain, it will hold the stock firmly against the rip fence. Using the fingerboard along with the push stick is the best—and safest—way to make an accurate rip.

whole thing together once it is cut in two. The advantage of this jig is that it supports the wood for its entire length and can be set up very accurately. Attaching two strips at 45-degree angles makes it superior for cutting picture frames. With modern multi-tooth carbide blades or hollow ground planer blades, perfect joints are easily obtained. In my own workshop, I can't remember the last time I used the miter gauge; it usually hangs on the wall collecting dust. It takes a little more wood, material, and care in design and execution, but it is possible to build a crosscut jig so that the guard splitter and anti-kickback paws do not have to be removed. This is worth the time because it allows you to quickly switch from crosscutting to ripping.

RIP FENCES

While the quality of the miter gauge is relatively unimportant, the quality of the rip fence is very important. Ripping is one of the most frequent uses of a table saw. The fence should be quick to operate and easy to adjust, and it should lock firm and parallel every time. Unfortunately, few saws, especially at the lower end of the price spectrum, meet these criteria. Even some of the add-on fences don't adjust easily. A very nice feature is a creeper control, most of which use a rack-and-pinion mechanism, to move the fence small amounts. Add-on T-square designs lack this feature and require constant pounding with a hand for neat adjustments. This can take its toll after a full day of work. The T-square designs are superior for people who cut a lot of plywood and large items. Unfortunately, there is little a user can do to improve a poor fence other than rip it off and install one of the add-on fences such as one offered by Biesmeyer. This is a very good way to upgrade a table saw.

ANGLE ADJUSTMENT

Most table saws have adjustments to tilt the blade between 90 degrees and 45 degrees to cut complicated angles and miters. Earlier saws did this by tilting the table. These days there are only a few saws left that use this design. Now, almost all table saws use a tilting arbor, which is unquestionably superior. The two saws I know of that still use tilting tables (Shopsmith and Inca) do so because they are really multi-purpose machines and have to accommodate other accessories. Whether the other accessories on the Shopsmith and the mortising machine of the Inca are worth the drawback of a tilting table is something that only the reader can answer. Both are well-built machines and offer some exciting versatility to the person with limited space.

HORSEPOWER

For 8- and 9-inch saws, 1 horsepower is adequate. However, 1½ horsepower is better. For 10- and 12-inch saws, 1½ horsepower is minimum and 2 to 3 horsepower is better, especially if you rip a lot of heavy hardwoods.

When buying a table saw, look at the motor and how it is mounted. Many table saws use motors designed specifically for that machine. This means a replacement motor must come from the manufacturer, and that can be more expensive than a generic motor. Although most motor rewinders can rebuild any motor, this factor is something to consider, especially if the company has long since gone out of business.

The other thing to look at is how power is transmitted. A few bigger industrial saws, especially in the 12-inch category, use direct drive. Most 8- or 10-inch saws use V-belts to transmit the power to the arbor. Generally speaking, the shorter the belt, the less the saw will vibrate. Also, it is usually better, especially on 2- and 3- horsepower saws, if power is transmitted by two or three matched belts. When replacing the belts, ensure that you get matched belts and not just off-the-shelf V-belts of the correct length. Matched belts are not readily available at hardware stores and usually have to be bought through industrial supply houses or bearing distribution companies.

GUARDS

Last, let's talk about guards. Unfortunately, most woodworkers tend to think of guards as an albatross foisted upon them by the Occupational Safety and Health Administration. This is far from the truth. I would not consider ripping a board without at least a kerf splitter and kickback paws in place. Almost any saw made within the last 15 or 20 years has these features. In a *Fine Woodworking* magazine survey of table saw accidents, no one had had an accident with these two items in place. This is food for thought, and emphasizes the need for extra care when guards must be removed to cut rabbets and dados. It is also why you should make push sticks before you ever plug your saw in. The plastic and metal guards that actually cover the blade are a mixed bag. They can give a false sense of security, especially to young operators in school shops, and I have seen really bad ones that caused more danger than they prevented.

Avoid guards that are cumbersome and need to be lifted frequently to accommodate wood. A guard should operate without ever having to put your hand near it. Again, there is a very good selection of fine add-on guards at fairly reasonable prices. If you buy a used saw with a bad guard or no guard at all, one of these should be obtained.

BAND SAW
Queen of the Power Tools

by W. Curtis Johnson

The table saw may be the king of the power tools, but the band saw is surely the queen. Unlike the king, which has a mind of his own, the queen is a gentle tool that leaves the user in control. She excels in cutting curves and resawing. I also prefer my band saw over the table saw for ripping, cross cuts, various angled cuts, and cutting end mortises and tenons.

The band saw is the mechanized version of the hand saw. Its continuous blade is stretched over two (or sometimes three) large wheels, one of which is driven by a motor. A second wheel can be adjusted to put tension on the blade and tilted to keep the blade tracking. A table, which can be tilted for angled cuts, provides a resting place for the wood. Most band saws can be outfitted wth a miter gauge and a fence, similar to those found on table saws. Two guide assemblies keep the blade running true, and ensure that the blade does move back as the wood is pushed through. One guide assembly is just under the table, while the second can be adjusted over the wood to be cut. Covers over the wheels and guards over the non-cutting portions of the blade protect the worker.

Like most woodworkers, I bought a table saw as my first power saw, but today, I would choose the band saw. I can see two reasons why beginners purchase a table saw. First, most beginners use plywood rather than lumber for their projects, and the table saw is certainly the power tool of choice for this material. Plywood can extend for any distance on either side of the blade, and the blade cuts cleanly enough for the joints used in plywood projects. Secondly, the table saw is more versatile. With a dado blade the table saw easily cuts the grooves and rabbets used in plywood joinery, although many dado blades do not perform well across the plywood grain. Moulding heads and sanding disks are also available for table saws.

With its gentler nature, the band saw is the queen of the power tools.

The band saw uses a continuous blade that is stretched over two large wheels. A table supplies support for the material. Although the wheel covers have been removed for this photo, it would be unsafe to use the saw without them.

The band saw excels at cutting curves.

I believe the band saw is the tool of choice when lumber is used to make fine furniture. Now resawing becomes an important procedure, and table saws do not resaw well. If the band saw is well tuned and has a sharp, high-quality blade, it will cross cut and rip with great accuracy. Curved cuts are often important, and a table saw will not cut curves. Tenons and 45° cuts are easily made on the band saw. None of these cuts will be as clean as the cuts on a table saw, but then a table saw cut will still not be clean enough for fine joinery anyway. When making furniture from lumber, long-grain edges should be planed, and cross-grain edges planed or sanded on a disk sander. Tenons should be cut slightly oversize, and reduced through planing for a perfect fit. Finally, the limiting throat of a band saw is usually not a problem when working with lumber. When the throat does get in the way of cross cutting, use a hand saw and then trim on the band saw.

It is true that a band saw is incapable of making grooves and rabbets, and shaping edges and surfaces, all of which are possible on a table saw. However, a router will perform these tasks and more, and is particularly easy to use if installed under a router table.

I love my little 14″ band saw. It is affordable, yet it is a quality tool that is large enough for all the operations I require. The wheels in this saw have the minimum diameter necessary to use standard band saw blades. If you try to use standard thickness blades on two or three wheel band saws with wheels less than 14″ in diameter, you will constantly deal with broken blades. The 14″ throat isn't very large, but the throat rarely gets in my way. The guide assemblies are not particularly fancy, but the metal blocks do an adequate job of holding the blade steady after they are tuned. I added a 6″ extension to give a full 12″ resaw capacity, and I do a lot of resawing on wide boards. This band saw will accept up to ¾″ blades, and I find ½″ blades quite large enough for resawing. I've added a miter gauge and a fence, both of which I use extensively. The worst feature of this saw is its small 14″ × 14″ table, but I've learned to live with that. The table does tilt 10° to the left as well as 45° to the right, and this left tilt is very useful when cutting dovetails.

Quality blades are essential for a band saw to perform properly. The dull blade of poor quality steel that came with my saw would hardly assure the purchaser that he had bought first-rate equipment. My local hardware store has an inexhaustible supply of these in various widths and teeth patterns. I am sure that poor quality and dull blades give the band saw a bad name, convincing woodworkers that the tool is not accurate. With sharp, quality blades, I never have trouble with blade wander, even when I resaw 12″ wide boards against a standard fence.

Quality blades with sharp, hardened teeth are available. You can mail order them directly from The Olson Saw Company (Bethel, CT 06801). This company also manufactures a line of the thin blades required for band saws with small wheels. Starrett blades are also first class, and are often sold by local power tool dealers. Most mail-order houses don't give the brand of their blades, but Woodcraft (P.O. Box 4000, Woburn, MA 01888) sells Starrett by name. My very favorite blades are made by Lenox. Instead of producing saw dust, these beauties produce little shavings. I don't know where you could mail order them. I buy mine from my local dealer in professional power tools (Western Tool Supply, 805 Burkhart SE, Albany, OR 97321). Undoubtedly, there are other companies that produce quality blades; these are the three with which I am familiar.

Resawing of wide lumber is particularly easy with a band saw. If the machine is well tuned and sports a sharp, quality blade, you can carry out this operation against a fence.

Band saw blades can be supplied in any length you might need, since the dealers simply weld a length from a roll to form the continuous band. Widths begin at 1/8″ and go up, although many dealers don't carry widths over ½″. The lore says that you should use as wide a blade as possible, because they are stiffer and can be used at a higher tension. In practice, I find that my ¾″ blades don't work any better than my ½″ blades and additionally, put a lot of strain on the saw. Another choice is the number of teeth per inch (TPI), which may vary from 32 to 2, depending on the type of tooth and the width of the blade. Both skip tooth and hook tooth patterns work equally well for me. I don't find that blades with more than 6 TPI are very useful for normal woodworking, because the irregularities at the weld and inaccuracies inherent in the machine limit the smoothness of the cut. However, blades with 10 or 12 TPI work better for thin material. Fewer TPI clear the chips better, and I often use a 3 TPI ½″ blade for resawing. However, my 6 TPI ½″ Lenox blade cuts so well, even for resawing wide boards, that I almost never remove it from the saw. A good selection for your shop would be a 1/8″ blade with 10 or 12 TPI; ¼″, 3/8″, and ½″ blades with 6 TPI; a ½″ blade with 3 TPI.

Like fan belts, band saw blades can be folded with one left-handed and one right-handed superturn so that they look like three small circles. I've seen long descriptions with pictures on how to do this, but I've never understood the point. Band saw blades do take up less room folded in this way, but scratches on the sides of the blades testify to the fact that the all-important teeth are being dulled. I just carefully hang all my blades on a large nail, and remove the entire pile to carefully separate them when I need another one. Band saw blades are often shipped folded, and I'm just happy to get them unfolded without damaging myself as they spring apart. *(AMEN! Ed.)*

As with most tools, band saws require tuning. Before purchasing the saw, check that the wheels are true by rotating the wheels with a blade installed. The blade should not shift from side to side in time with the wheels. If a saw you own has an out-of-true wheel, you can rotate the wheel and use a piece of sandpaper glued to a fixed piece of wood to remove high spots from the rubber tire. The wheels should also be well balanced. With the blade removed, see if either wheel always settles with the same side down. If so, remove metal from the low, heavy side until the wheel is balanced.

The guide assemblies are the most important part to true, and may require a lot of work if your side supports are hardened metal blocks that rub against the blade. First, square the ends of the blocks to their sides (one block has a 45° miter on my saw). Since the blocks are exceedingly hard, this will require mechanical grinding against a stone designed for flat work. Next, rotate the guide assemblies so the side supports contact the blade over their entire surface. You may well have to file the holes that hold the blocks to achieve perfect contact for both blocks. Adjust one block so that it kisses the blade. Then adjust the other block so the blade just slides through. The directions that came with my saw call for a fair amount of play, but in my opinion, play equal to the thickness of a sheet of paper is too much. I like a minimum of play to keep the blade running true, and have never had trouble with anything overheating or the hardened blocks wearing. However, I often have to clean up sloppy welds with a grinder or hand stone so that the weld will run between the side supports. Truing this type of guide can be time consuming, so if you have more money than time, you may wish to purchase all ball bearing guides from your dealer as a retrofit. The set of ball bearings to the rear of the blade should be adjusted so the free blade just misses them. Now move the side supports forward so they are just behind the gullets between the teeth of the blade.

Even though my band saw sits on a cheap sheet metal stand, it still passes Frank Pittman's nickel test (*Woodworkers Buyer's Guide to Power Tools*, JM Publications, P.O. Box 1408,

The blade of a band saw pushes against the table, so you are always in control. I use my little machine for all my ripping, but I keep my fingers well away from the blade.

The band saw will cross cut as well as a table saw, although the cut will not be quite as smooth.

Hendersonville, TN 37077). That is only because I spent a lot of time tuning the pulley system. The large pot metal pulley on the driven wheel was far from true, and I replaced it with a quality cast iron pulley from my local automotive store. I also bought a flexible seamless belt. The motor was adjusted so that the belt was perfectly straight from drive pulley to driven pulley. I got the best results with minimal tension on the belt. Now a nickel will stand tall on the table with the motor running. Certainly a sturdier stand (perhaps a home-built wooden one) and sand bags would improve things even more, but I like the flexibility of having casters available on my saw.

Next you can round and smooth the edges of the table with a bench stone. Cast iron is too hard for a file. Adjust the table so the miter gauge groove is parallel to the width of the blade. Put a straight edge against a 3 TPI ½″ blade where the set of the tooth is away from the straight edge, and measure to the groove. Since band saw blades are narrow, this adjustment is not highly accurate, but it need not be particularly accurate for the same reason. If necessary, raise the insert at the blade to the level of the table with a few layers of masking tape. Finally, adjust the table so it is perpendicular to the length of the blade. This can be very accurate if you put a light behind the saw and view the blade's teeth against a square.

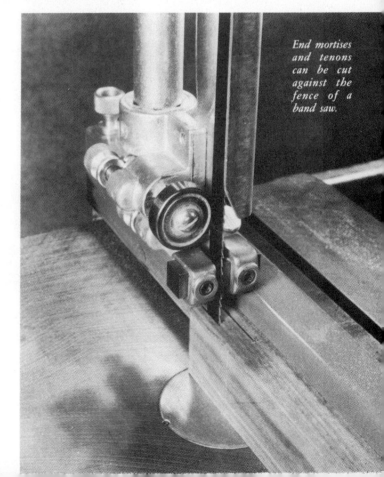

End mortises and tenons can be cut against the fence of a band saw.

If you have purchased a miter gauge and fence for your band saw, these should also be adjusted. The miter gauge stops at 90° (marked 0° on some gauges) and 45° are most accurately set by trial and error cuts on an 8″ wide board. The fence should be adjusted so that the inside is parallel to the miter gauge slot. It is also important for the fence to be perpendicular to the table for resawing. I had to do some filing on the front clamp block to accomplish this adjustment. You may also want to rig up special lighting to better see your work.

Cross cutting, ripping, and curve cutting are all straightforward operations. Since the saw blade pushes directly against the table, you are always in control. The saw will not grab the wood and throw it, as sometimes happens with a table saw. However, don't be fooled by the band saw's gentler nature. It is completely indiscriminate as to what material it is cutting. Keep your fingers away from the blade and use push sticks. Always lower the guide post so the assembly is ¼ to ½″ above the material being cut.

Most of this work can be performed with ½″ wide blades, but for curves you may need to go to a narrower blade that is consistent with the radius of the tightest curve. The approximate minimum radius for a band saw blade is three times its width.

Resawing requires the most accurate set up. The table must be perpendicular to the blade, and the fence parallel to the blade over both its length and width. I added an extension to increase the size of my fence when resawing especially wide boards. Plane the edge of the material that will be against the table perpendicular to the face that will be against the fence. It pays to mark the top edge of the board at the resaw point so you can compensate for minor errors in the setup and in the straightness of the lumber. As I've stated before, a ½″ wide blade will work just fine if it is sharp

and has only a few teeth per inch. Feed lightly and let the blade clear the large amount of saw dust it is generating in this procedure. With a little care, you will be surprised how well a small band saw will resaw wide boards against a fence.

Other operations that work well on the band saw are cutting end mortises and tenons, nibbling out material between tenons, and cutting edges or ends at an angle. Ripping the faces of end mortises and tenons is similar to resawing and can be done against the fence. Cross cut with the miter gauge to form the shoulders. Nibbling out material between two points can be done with the fence on the throat side of the blade to maintain an accurate depth. Modern woodworkers are not used to tilting tables for cutting angled edges, but I've come to prefer them over the tilting arbor of a table saw. It is certainly a lot faster to loosen a nut and tilt the table than to crank over the arbor of a table saw. I find it easy to control the boards on a tilted table, and when the cut involves the fence, gravity keeps the board nestled nicely in the V between the fence and the table.

I hope that I have ably conveyed the reasons for my love affair with the queen of the power tools. I feel much safer using this machine, and I now rarely use my table saw. The ability of the band saw to resaw wide lumber allows me to glue up 24″ boards that have perfectly book-matched grain. As with other tools, the keys to success are tuning of the machine and using sharp cutting edges. With the band saw, the router, and the hand planes I have discussed here in *The American Woodworker*, it is possible to build a lot of fine furniture from coarse looking lumber.

ABOUT THE AUTHOR:

W. Curtis Johnson is a contributing editor to **The American Woodworker.**

It is possible to nibble away the wood between two tenons using a band saw and its fence to define the depth.

Choosing The Right Band Saw Blade

by B. William Bigelow

Select the right band saw blade for the job, put it on a tuned and balanced band saw, and the cutting performance will please the best of us. The best band saw will not cut well without the proper blade, nor will the best blade last long on an improperly adjusted machine. The marriage between the band saw blade and the band saw must be a good one to last.

The first band saw blade I took notice of came on a used 14″ Powermatic. What a peach of a machine! It was well balanced, with fine castings, and cut beautifully. At the time I was only contour sawing in ¾″ stock and occasionally replaced the four tooth per inch skip tooth blade. All seemed well in the world.

A few years later, when I was wiser and much poorer, I swapped some cordwood for a used and maladjusted Sears 12″ band saw. The wheels were out of round, the guide blocks missing, and the tires similar to those on my old car. As soon as I got the band saw to cease hopping around the shop, I turned my attention to band saw blades. By this time I wanted to resaw, cut green wood cylinders, cut jointwork, and saw through any wood, thick and thin. As my experience had grown, so had my curiosity. The time had come for a little knowledge on band saw blades.

Band saw blades are selected by length, width, pitch, tooth style, set, as well as metal thickness and type. Each of these characteristics will help determine the best blade for the job. These variables may at first suggest the band saw owner needs a closet full of blades. In practice, however, most craftsmen need only three or four different blades for all their cutting needs. Once the terms are understood, blade selection is easy. *Figure 1.*

BLADE LENGTH

The first step is to determine the length of the blade for the machine. Band saw length, as well as the machine size, varies from the different band saw manufacturers, but fortunately the information is easy to come by. The blade length may be in the owner manual, stamped on the machine, or on the box from the previous blade. If this fails, or to double check, calculate the length from the formula in *Figure 2.* Before measuring the distance between the wheel centers, MAKE SURE THE TENSIONING ADJUSTMENT IS RELAXED.

BLADE WIDTH

The blade width is the distance from the teeth tip to the back of the blade. *Figure 3.* Choose the widest blade possible for the job. If you are sawing straight cuts, choose the widest blade the band saw will handle. For curved cuts, choose the widest blade that will make the curve.

Band saw blades survive a lot of torture. The constant flexing of metal over the wheels produces heat and metal fatigue. So does twisting and bowing from feed pressure and the cutting table. Friction and heat at the teeth tips add to shorten blade life. Engineers have come up with metal characteristics to combat these early retirement forces.

Often much is said about the cutting teeth of the band saw blade and little about the body of the blade. Yet the blade may break long before the teeth become dull. The body of the blade must flex and straighten continuously under tension. Steel used in the band saw is carbon steel or spring steel tempered to flex. Small band saws, especially three wheel band saws, are hardest on blades. Their small diameter wheels flex the steel in a tighter radius and more frequently than the wheels of the larger saws. To handle this increased stress band saw manufacturers must use thinner steel for small band saw blades. Most small (length) blades are also of spring steel. Flexibility has its price, however. Thin flexible steel is not as strong and can not take the tension that the thicker metal can. The small band saw blades will break under the tension put on the larger band saws.

Using the widest blade possible for the job will allow the blade to be tensioned higher. Wide blades are stronger and have more metal to resist stretching. The trick is to get the blade as tight and stiff as the metal will allow without excessive metal fatigue and breakage. The stiff and tense metal will wobble and bow less, and cut smoother.

As stock is fed into the moving blade, the feed pressure pushes the blade backward into the upper and lower guide wheels of the band saw. The blade tends to bow backwards between the supporting guide wheels. This bow, if excessive, wears the blade, and negatively affects

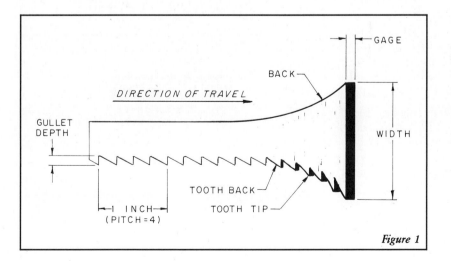

GAGE

BACK

DIRECTION OF TRAVEL

GULLET DEPTH

WIDTH

TOOTH BACK

TOOTH TIP

1 INCH
(PITCH=4)

Figure 1

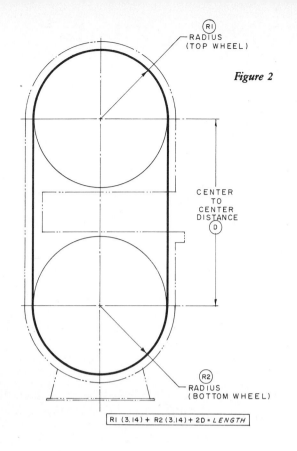

RADIUS
(TOP WHEEL)

Figure 2

CENTER
TO
CENTER
DISTANCE
(D)

R2
RADIUS
(BOTTOM WHEEL)

R1 (3.14) + R2 (3.14) + 2D = *LENGTH*

TOOTH, like the skip tooth, has large gullets, but the rake angle is increased to 10 degrees. The hook tooth is an aggressive self feeder, pulling itelf into the stock. The increase in rake angle reduces feed pressure and consequent bowing of the blade, but because the blade will wobble more, the cut will not be as smooth as the other tooth styles.

One of the biggest complaints regarding band saw blades is that they do not track well. The blade tends to wander to the left or right. Wander is common enough that all good resaw fences are adjustable to compensate for the individual blade wander. If the saw blade has perfect set and the teeth tips project equally from the body of the blade, the blade should not wander. Some manufacturers (Olympia Saw) guarantee saw set to .002 inch. It is not difficult, however, to ruin set in use. If the teeth on one side of the blade dull on a hard object such as a nail or hard knot, the blade will wander. Frequently, hard turns (especially with thin blades) will ruin set. Recognizing differences in the cutting characteristics of individual saw blades, I often set the perfect blade aside for my best work.

PITCH = TPI

Pitch is defined as the number of teeth per inch. The number of teeth per inch selected for the job varies with the hardness and thickness of the stock and the speed of the band saw blade. The greater number of teeth engaged

Figure 3

WIDTH

Figure 4

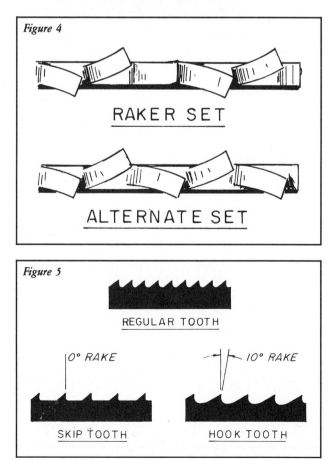

RAKER SET

ALTERNATE SET

cutting accuracy. Using a wide blade will decrease the bow, because the blade is stronger. Another very easy way to reduce bow is to lower the top guide wheels to just above the stock being cut. Aside from being an excellent safety practice, this adjustment will reduce the SPAN of the unsupported blade between the guide wheels. Hence, the bow will be less and the blades will last longer.

BLADE TEETH

Band saw blades, like a hand saw, have teeth bent to each side of the body of the blade. Bending of the teeth to the sides is called set, and it is done to make the saw cut wider than the body of the blade. Setting the saw teeth to the left and right of the blade will cut a wide enough kerf to allow plenty of room for the blade to follow without binding. The kind of radius the band saw will cut is primarily dependent on the size of the kerf and the width of the blade to follow. A narrow blade with a wide kerf will literally "turn circles" around a wide blade with a small kerf.

Two popular types of set are called raker and alternate set. On raker set, one tooth is bent to the left, one to the right , the third tooth is left unset, and the pattern repeats. On alternate set, one tooth is bent to the left, and one to the right. *Figure 4.*

Three styles (or shapes) of teeth are commonly available in woodworking blades. *Figure 5.* The REGULAR tooth style has teeth and gullets the same size with zero degree rake. It is best for smooth cuts in thin materials. The teeth are so close together they tend to clog in thick materials. The SKIP TOOTH blade was designed for faster cuts in thicker materials. As the name implies, every other tooth is missing and the gullets become big enough for large chip removal. The skip tooth, like the regular tooth, has a zero degree rake angle and scrapes the chip from the stock. The HOOK

REGULAR TOOTH

0° RAKE

10° RAKE

SKIP TOOTH

HOOK TOOTH

Figure 5

(I recommend at least three) with the stock at the same time will yield the smoothest cuts. For thin stock ten or more teeth per inch is recommended. Wide resawing blades have two to three teeth per inch, where as general cutting blades use four to six teeth per inch.

Heat, as well as abrasion, is a prime enemy of teeth tips. The right combination of feed speed (stock advancing into the blade), blade speed (measured in feet per minute), and the pitch of the blade will keep the teeth cool. The best combination of these factors forces the tooth to take a moderate chip without rubbing the wood into a slow burn. If the band saw speed is adjustable, slow the blade speed in thick stock. My band saw is not easily adjustable (running at 3,000 surface feet per minute), but I can change the feed speed and the pitch by installing different blades. In stock over 2″ thick I use four or less teeth per inch with wide gullets. The widely spaced teeth and large gullets cut into the stock without gumming and building excessive heat. Controlling the stock feed is primarily a matter of experience. If stock is pushed into the blade too fast, accuracy and quality of the cut will suffer. Excessive speed breaks blades. On the other hand, too slow of speed will burn the wood and heat the teeth tips. Probably all of us have experienced burning at one time or another, such as when we are concentrating on accuracy and creep too slowly into the work.

WELDING

Resharpening saw blades used to be a lot more common than it is today. I find the time spent in grinding blades not very cost effective. The money saved will not pay my wages for the time spent. If one evaluates his / her time differently, blades can be reground and set several times over. Jigs and fixtures can be made to position the blade during regrinding.

No article on band saw blades could be complete without some information on the welding process. Band saw blades are manufactured in large rolls, then cut to smaller rolls (usually 250′), or welded into loops. Most band saw owners buy pre-welded loops for convenience. The blade is ordered by length and the dealer cuts and welds to the length specified. Since each loop is custom welded I would not hesitate to purchase a band saw with an "odd ball length of blade". The band is cut square and flash butt welded. The weld itself is not as tricky as the alignment process. The loop must flow smoothly without the weld bumping. There is some cost savings in buying rolls and welding loops if the equipment is available.

I also buy pre-welded loops for convenience. In time, I've had a share of broken loops hung on the wall; many with sharp teeth. The blades, more often than not, seem to break on the welds. Although quality control is usually very good, manufacturers have, from time to time, had trouble in this area. As I operate a shop for beginners, I suspect many failures must be caused by our mishandling as well. So what to do with the broken loops? New Milford Specialties (24A South Main St., New Milford, CT 06776), also a dealer in Olson band saw blades, supplied us with a silver brazing kit for testing. I found the directions easy to read and the brazing process simple to master. The kit comes with an alignment jig, silver solder, flux, and directions. A propane torch is required for heat. The broken blade ends are ground to a scarf angle (I used the same 30 degree jig we use on plane irons), aligned in the jig, and silver soldered. To date, we have been able to use our inventory of broken blades with satisfactory results.

METALLURGY

Whatever is said about metallurgy is truly a very little about a lot of research. Carbon steel used in most of the woodworking blades is tempered for flex and later the teeth are heat hardened for long wear. The teeth are too hard to file and must be ground if resharpening is attempted. Spring steel is often used when more flex is required. The teeth in spring steel are also hardened. Contour Saw (Olympia Brand) markets a Spring-Bak (trade name) band saw which can be tensioned higher than their carbon steel blade and longer life is claimed. Lenox markets among their saw blades a bi-metal blade. A strip of cobalt steel is electro welded to a spring steel back. Although the bi-metal blade is more expensive, the cobalt steel teeth can stand more heat and the blade a greater tension than carbon steel.

THE RIGHT CHOICE

A wide variety of cutting requirements suggest several different blades for the band saw. If, on the other hand, the band saw is relegated to only one type of cutting, perhaps one blade type is all that is needed. In our general all around shop I maintain a 20″ Powermatic band saw and an inventory of four different blades. The wheels of the band saw are most familiar with a 3 / 8″, 4 TPI hook tooth blade. This is a fine combination for all around cutting. When tight turns are attempted I switch to a ¼″, 4 TPI blade. Even the ¼″ blade is tensioned as high as I can, because I often cut through up to 12″ of green oak in tight circles. Resawing is done with a 1″, ¾ TPI skip tooth blade. I also stock ¼″, 14 TPI regular toothed blades but they are seldom used. They fail to be installed on the band saw because of the availability of a scroll saw in the shop. The band saw is, I believe, the saw of greatest versatility. With a good selection of blades and a well tuned machine, it is my choice of saws.

ABOUT THE AUTHOR:
B. William Bigelow is a contributing editor to **The American Woodworker.**

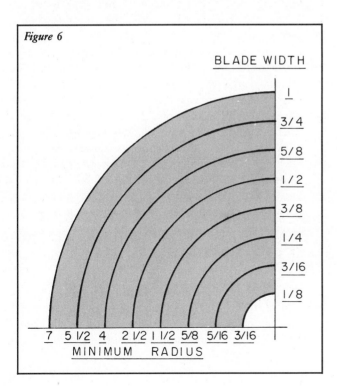

Figure 6

BLADE WIDTH

1
3/4
5/8
1/2
3/8
1/4
3/16
1/8

7   5 1/2   4   2 1/2   1 1/2   5/8   5/16   3/16
MINIMUM   RADIUS

The Answer: Jointers and Planers

Editor's note: *The following discussion of jointers and planers is from "The Answer," a column by Ernie Conover that appeared regularly in* American Woodworker.

I'll be discussing jointers and planers together because these tools are designed to work as a team. Many people seem to be confused about the true purpose of these machines, so let's start with a brief explanation.

The purpose of a jointer is to get a surface really flat. It removes all the irregularities inherent in wood: cup, warp, and wind. But a jointer cannot make a second side parallel to the first. That is the job of the planer. Both machines are necessary to obtain flat S-4-S (surfaced four sides) lumber suitable for cabinet work.

THE JOINTER

The jointer is a simple machine, but must be well made if it is going to do superlative work. It consists of two tables separated by a cutter head and arranged so that they always remain in the same plane. On cheaper machines, only the infeed table is movable, while on better machines both tables are adjustable. A movable outfeed table is very important. Its main asset is that it can be quickly adjusted to the same height as the cutter head, which saves a lot of time in a production shop. The main considerations are that the tables are solid and that they actuate smoothly without play.

The best way to check that the tables are parallel is to place a straightedge on the outfeed table and a small piece (about 1 inch square) of wood under it on the infeed table. Run the table up until the wood just touches the straightedge. Now see how the block fits under the straightedge at several points along the infeed table. Repeat the process at the same setting at each edge of the jointer table. If the jointer passes this inspection, both tables are in the same plane. In longer (50-inch to 75-inch) jointers, run-outs of up to about .006 inch are normal and acceptable. In smaller machines .004 inch is an acceptable tolerance.

JOINTER CUTTER HEADS

Jointer cutter heads are pretty simple. There are a lot of older machines on the market that have knives that bolt directly to the cutter head. These are called square head machines and should be avoided because they are very hard to adjust. The more modern wedge head, where the knife is held in a pocket by the wedging action of a row of bolts in a gib, is much easier to adjust and maintain. A radius in the gib also acts as a chip breaker. A three-knife cutter head is nice, but two-knife heads are quite adequate and cost less. Look for a cutter head speed of at least 5,000 rpm.

FENCES

One of the most important features in a jointer is the fence. Many buyers carefully check that the tables are flat to .0001 inch and completely overlook the fence. It should be as straight and true as the table, and have plenty of adjustment. Search for adjustments that are positive and easy to use. Some better jointers can skew the fence across the tables. This can help greatly when jointing difficult woods such as curly maple. Lateral adjustment is a must so that the wear of edge jointing can be distributed evenly along the cutter head. Positive but adjustable stops at 90 to 45 degrees are a time-saving convenience.

Many jointers have a rabbeting ledge. The fence is moved all the way to the left for this operation and the guard generally has to be removed. For this reason, rabbeting is somewhat dangerous. Since there are so many other ways to rabbet today, I am not sure this feature is any longer important.

JOINTER HORSEPOWER

Jointers don't require much horsepower because the motor only drives the cutter head and the user provides the power to move the material. Three-quarters of a horsepower is ample for small machines up to 6 inches. Two or 3 horsepower is ample for 8- and 12-inch machines, and no jointer needs more than 5 horsepower.

Finally, jointers can be real man-eaters, rating right at the top of the list of dangerous tools. Guards help, but nothing beats care and common sense. Use push sticks, and never joint anything shorter than 6 inches. Never stack work on the jointer table, because when it falls the natural reaction is to grab for it.

The guard used almost universally today in front of the cutter head is the so-called "boomerang" type. This is a crescent-shaped guard that is pushed out of the way by the wood, but springs back to cover the cutter head. When the fence is moved laterally, a boomerang guard moves accordingly and does its job, but the cutter head is now exposed in back of the fence. It is easy to lose a finger to this exposed area because all attention is on the work going on in front of the fence. Guarding in back of the fence is helpful, but common sense and training will avoid this type of accident. A back guard is easy to fabricate yourself from wood and an old hinge.

THE PLANER

The rotary-head planer dates from the Woodworth pattern of 1828. This basic patent was for planing wood by forcing a plank under a high speed revolving cutter head with feeding rollers. Woodworth vociferously defended his patent

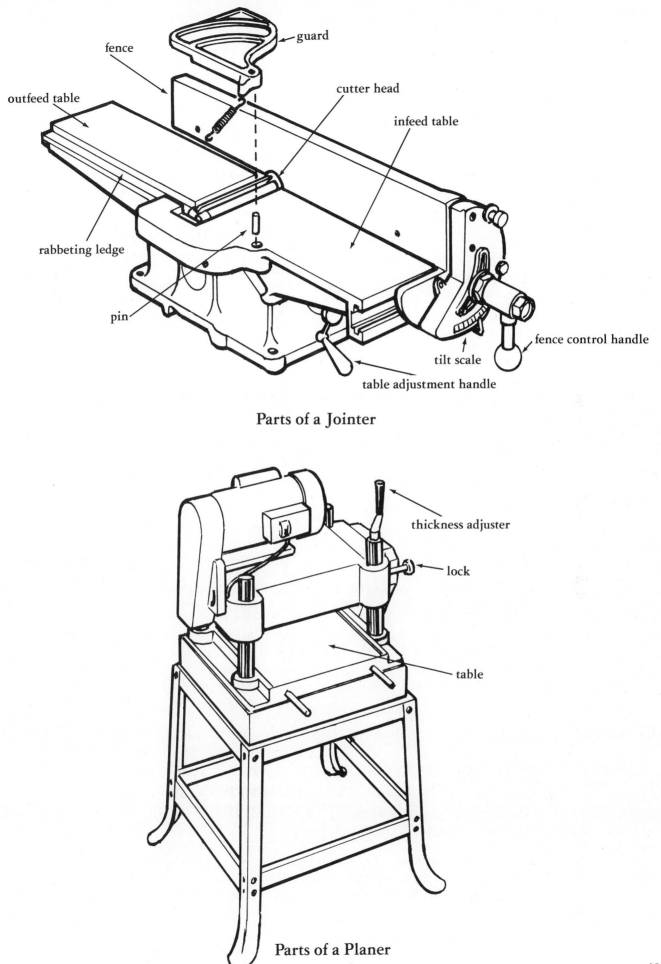

Parts of a Jointer

Parts of a Planer

and for many years put all lookalikes out of business. The only other planer until about 1850 was the Danels patent of 1835. In this design, the work was dogged down on a moving bed. The bed then moved under a revolving fly cutter much like a rotary lawn mower. The tool cut in an arc across the surface of the board. The Danels planer took up a lot of space, for the moving bed was enormous. Sharpened properly, it left a board that was both jointed and planed with a very good finish. With modern super high speed carbide tooling, I have often wondered why the Danels planer has not been revived.

Today, virtually all the woodworking planers built world-wide use the basic principles of the Woodworth patent with many innovations and improvements. Let's look at what the various factors and features are and how we can tell a good planer from a bad one.

PLANER CUTTER HEADS

The heart of any planer is the cutter head. The original Woodworth machine used a square head design, and there are still a few square head machines in operation and available on the used market. The square head gets its name from the fact that the knives are bolted to flat spots milled on the head. Without the knives in place, the head looks square rather than cylindrical. Though some claim that square heads are dangerous, I disagree; they are just very hard to set.

All modern planers use the wedge head design in which the knife is held tightly in a trapezoidal pocket by a gib and a series of bolts. The knives are much quicker to change and set in a wedge head. Another advantage is that a small radius can be placed in the gib to act as a chip breaker much like the cap iron in a hand plane. The proximity of this radius to the knife edge is critical in difficult woods; however, as the distance diminishes, the ability to take heavy cuts diminishes proportionately.

Cutter heads can have two, three, and sometimes four knives. Two-knife cutter heads, are, naturally, cheapest and usually are restricted to light, commercial, and home work-shop planers. Two-knife cutter heads work well, but you must sharpen blades more often because each blade is doing more work. Also, a two-knife cutter head must turn faster or the wood must be fed proportionately slower to get acceptable finishes.

BED DESIGN

On most modern planers, the bed moves up and down under the cutter head. There are a few designs in which the cutter head moves up and down, but these seem harder to work out. The distance between the cutter head and the bed controls the thickness of the material being planed. There are many methods of raising and lowering the bed, but the most common is using jack screws operated by a hand wheel or, on larger planers, an electric motor. On cheaper home workshop planers, the material often rides directly on the bed and these types of planers require quite a bit more horsepower because of

the need to overcome the friction. Better planers use an idling bed roller on either side of the cutter head.

BED ROLLERS

The bed rollers have an adjustment so that they can be raised or lowered in relation to the bed, and generally are set about $1/64$ to $1/16$ inch above the surface of the bed. The lower setting is for finish work while the higher setting is used for rough-sawn lumber. The idling bed rollers allow material to actually roll rather than rest directly on the bed, thus eliminating a great deal of friction. Cheaper planers use very small-diameter rollers with oil sleeves or no bearings. Better machines use ball bearings. The problem with small-diameter bed rollers is that they tend to drop into holes in rough-sawn lumber and create more problems than if they weren't there at all. Another nice feature, which is available on many planers today, is a quick cam-type adjustment for raising and lowering the bed rollers. This allows changing from finish-work height to rough-sawn height simply by flicking a lever rather than a time-consuming series of adjustments.

FEED ROLLERS

Above each bed roller is a feed roller. Traditionally, the feed rollers are of cast iron, and the infeed roller is serrated, while the outfeed roller is smooth. The serrated infeed roller is necessary to grip the wood and propel it through the cutter head, especially on the initial cut where the surface often is uneven. Better machines use a segmented infeed roller in which the roller is divided into small segments or cells that float in relation to a concentric central shaft. The advantage to the segmented infeed roller is that it will get a good grip on an odd-shaped board on the initial cut so that it does not wander or turn under the cutter head. This is also a great advantage when planing a lot of narrow strips. It allows the strips to be fed side by side but at equal rates of speed. Without a segmented infeed roller, the thickest work will feed first. In the last few years, a great many light commercial and home workshop planers have gone to rubber-covered feed rollers. These rollers grip the work well and eliminate the need for a serrated infeed roller. They also act somewhat like a segmented roller; however, they are not as good as the real McCoy. A few older machines on the market have driven bed rollers as well as feeding rollers above. These machines make for terrific feeding.

CHIPPERS AND PRESSURE BARS

The next items to look at in the planer are the chipper and the pressure bar. The chipper is a device that rides on the surface of the wood between the infeed roller and the cutter head. It performs the very important function of holding down the wood in front of the cutter head and preventing tear-out.

Chippers are necessary in planing difficult woods where reverse and wild grain are prevalent. They act much like the sole on a hand plane, and their proximity to the cutter head is important. On better machines, the chippers also are segmented like the infeed roller so they will ride uniformly across the surface and do the job despite the difficult situation. It must be remembered, however, that after the initial pass, when the board is trued up, the presence of segmented chippers is of no consequence. For this reason, the value of chippers may be overrated, because one seldom brings lumber to its final dimension in one pass, especially on smaller machines.

A pressure bar does exactly the same job as a chipper. But instead of riding on the wood between the infeed roller and the cutter head, a pressure bar rides on the wood between the cutter head and the outfeed roller. Because the wood is planed coming out of the cutter head, there is no reason for the pressure bar to be segmented.

One other thing chippers and damper bars do is dampen vibration in the wood during planing.

Chippers and pressure bars usually are not found on home workshop and light commercial machines. They are found only on the better and heavier industrial cast iron machines.

FEED RATE AND SPEED

There is much debate in the industry about what is the best rate of feed, whether the feed rate needs to be variable, and cuts per inch. All these factors are interdependent and vary greatly with the diameter of the cutter head, which complicates the picture. We have to speak in generalities, but it is safe to say that the larger the diameter of the cutter head, the better. A large circumscribed radius leaves less rippling on the wood, and the feed rate and speed of the cutter head should be configured to yield a minimum of about 40 cuts per inch. Most machines sold today yield a minimum of 50 cuts per inch. The formula to derive cuts per inch is as follows: cutter head speed times the number of knives in the cutter head, divided by the feed rate, multiplied by 12. This will yield the number of cuts per inch.

Now we come to the controversy over variable rates of feed. Although this is certainly a nice feature to have, I'm not sure it is something that should negate the purchase of a particular planer. Generally speaking, reducing the feed rate only produces marginal increases in finish quality. It is a feature that can be useful to someone who constantly works with very exotic woods.

PLANER HORSEPOWER

Generally, a planer can't have too much horsepower. Most 12-inch machines need a minimum of 3 horsepower, and preferably 5 if they lack bed rollers. Machines in the 18-inch range need a minimum of 5 horsepower and more if they have babbet bearings or driven bed rollers. Machines in the 24- and 36-inch range need at least 7½ to 10 horsepower.

SHARPENING

A sought-after feature in planers is the ability to sharpen knives in the cutter head. This is done by a little grinding machine, similar to a tool post grinder for a lathe, which can be positioned over the cutter head to hone the knives. This certainly is a useful machine in shops where frequent sharpening is necessary. It should be realized that this type of grinding machine only hones an edge and will not actually regrind the entire bevel angle. Knives still must be removed periodically for regrinding. A serious drawback to in-the-machine sharpening is that the knives have to be set to protrude from the cutter head a good distance. This makes the distance to the chip-breaking radius in the gib and the chipper a compromise. Consequently, performance may suffer in difficult planing situations.

Thanks to the Occupational Safety and Hazard Administration, planer designers have become greatly concerned with noise. As a result, many designers have gone to spiral cutter heads. The cutter head has a spiral knife and is actually much like a spirally fluted metal milling cutter. A great disadvantage to this type of planer is that sharpening can be done only by a highly professional service. The advantage is that they have a much lower noise level and can produce a better finish because of the shearing nature of the spiral cut as opposed to the rather abrupt nature of a straight-bladed planer knife.

ADJUSTMENT

When buying a planer, remember that ease of adjustment is an important part of performance. This is because a planer requires frequent adjustment to provide top performance. Pride of ownership soon will be lost on a machine that is difficult to adjust and maintain. On the other hand, a machine that is simple to adjust and maintain is a joy to own.

Setting Jointer Knives

By Thomas W. Miller

Using a jointer that has sharp knives and is adjusted perfectly is one of the joys of woodworking — every edge is perfectly straight and the surface is as smooth as silk.

Likewise, using a jointer with dull knives or one that is out of adjustment ruins nearly everything that it touches. The edges can't be glued together and the surface is so rough that it feels like a washboard. If a fine-tuned jointer is so desirable and the alternative so awful, why are so many woodworking shops being held hostage by bad jointers?

The answer lies in the fact that all too many woodworkers do not know how jointer knives should be set, and if they do, they can't seem to get the knives set the way they know they should be. Hopefully, this article will explain how knives are supposed to be set and how to get them set accurately and safely.

Essentially, setting knives in a cutterhead is simply a matter of getting them all the same in height and even on one end if rabbeting is to be done. The cutting circle is the path that the cutting edge follows as the cutterhead rotates. If all knives are set on exactly the same cutting circle, they will extend into the wood by exactly the same amount and each knife will do the same amount of cutting. If the knives are also being set for rabbeting, then all of the ends on the outside end must also be matched. Also, the top of the cutting circle must be in exactly the same plane as the outfeed table.

An early word of caution: jointer knives are extremely sharp and will readily cut fingers at the slightest slip during the process of changing knives. Do not use your hands in such a way that if something slides, slips, or suddenly becomes loose your fingers or hands would move toward or slide along the cutting edge.

Jointer Type

All jointers have an infeed table that is adjustable to set the depth of cut for each pass. However, not all outfeed tables are adjustable. Since the top of the cutting circle must be in exactly the same plane as the outfeed table, you must either set the knives to be exactly right for the outfeed table, or you can set the knives and then adjust the outfeed table to the proper relationship. Obviously, adjusting the outfeed table after the knives have been set is much easier.

The first thing that you must do before setting jointer knives is to determine if the outfeed table on the jointer is stationary or adjustable. With that determination, you can proceed, keeping in mind to use the following instructions that pertain to your type of jointer.

Cutterheads

There are two basic types of jointer cutterheads: heads with bolt-on knives and heads with knives set in machined slots.

Cutterheads with bolt-on type knives usually have slots in the knives with the tightening bolts going through the knife slots and into the cutterhead body. The knife is secured simply by tightening down the bolts and adjustments are made by loosening the bolts and repositioning the knives. Usually this type of cutterhead only carries two knives and sometimes there is a clamping type device that fits between the knives and the heads of the securing bolts.

Cutterheads with knife slots are more popular today and usually carry three and sometimes four knives. The knife is secured in place by a 'knife-tightening gibb' (see illustration). The gibb sets in front of the knife and contains a row of square-head screws that are threaded into the gibb. As the gibb screws are backed out of the gibb, they press against the back of the knife slot and force the gibb against the knife. The knife is squeezed between the gibb and the side of the cutterhead slot, thereby being securely held in place. The biggest mistake that is made with this type of cutterhead is trying to loosen the knives by unscrewing the gibb screws. Remember, the knives are loosened by screwing the gibb screws *into* the gibb (toward the knife). This is exactly opposite the natural tendency, but countless wrenches have been broken, squarehead bolts have been rounded, and fingers have been cut trying to back these screws out to loosen the knives.

A convenience feature on some cutterheads that is very easy to learn to like is knife elevating screws in the cutterhead (see illustration). They are simply a little plug set into the cutterhead with a notch for the knife and an Allen screw running through the middle. By rotating the Allen screw, you incremently raise or lower the knife. Knives are much easier to set to extremely close tolerances with this feature.

Without the knife-elevating screws, raising the knife a precise amount is both frustrating and difficult. If you have room to get a little screwdriver under the end of the knife to pry against the bottom of the knife slot, the knife can be raised, although not very precisely. Some people have ground an Allen wrench to fit under the end of the knife to act as a pry bar. Lowering knives is much simpler; they are easily driven into the cutterhead with taps from a piece of wood or some other soft object that will not damage the knife edge.

Jointer Nomenclature

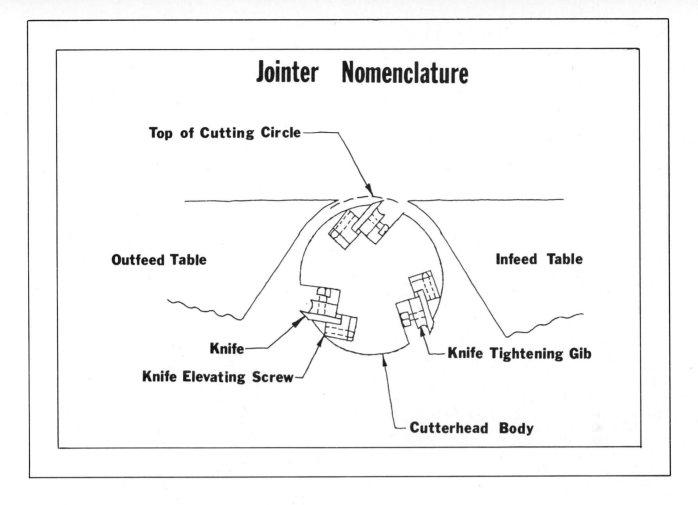

Top of Cutting Circle

Outfeed Table

Infeed Table

Knife

Knife Tightening Gib

Knife Elevating Screw

Cutterhead Body

On all cutterheads it is much better to remove and replace one knife at a time than to remove all of the knives at once. This is especially true for cutterheads with the tightening gibs for securing the knives because with the other knives still in place and tight, the forces within the cutterhead will be more in balance.

Dial Indicator

The dial indicator is the most accurate device for setting jointer knives—and it is considerably easier to use if it has a magnetic base. *(For those who like to be different, see the article "Jointer Knife Adjuster" in the September 1985 issue of* American Woodworker.*)* The indicator itself should have a movement range of about .250 inch to facilitate in setting any height differential you may desire. When using a dial indicator for this purpose, the round body of the cutterhead is used as the standard that all measurements are taken from. The knives are set a given distance above the surface of the cutterhead body. This given distance is determined in one of the following ways depending upon what type of outfeed table your jointer has.

If the outfeed table is not adjustable, then you must first determine the measurement between the top center of the round cutterhead and the surface of the outfeed table as follows: First, with the magnet off, set the indicator on the outfeed table and adjust the indicator point so that it is perpendicular to the table and the dial reads zero. Then slide the base over to the front edge of the outfeed table and sweep the indicator point across the cutterhead body to determine the highest point on the cutterhead body. Now the difference between the zero reading on the outfeed table and the reading at the top of the cutterhead is the exact measurement that the knives must be set above the cutterhead.

If your jointer outfeed table is adjustable, everything is considerably easier. All you have to do is determine how much you want your knives to extend above the cutterhead and set them all at that number. A nice round number is easier to find on a dial indicator and I usually use either .100 inch or .125 inch.

The dial indicator can be set just about any place while setting knives: infeed table, outfeed table, fence, or anywhere handy. It can be moved as often as you want during the process and requires no particular accuracy in placing the base prior to taking measurements since it is only measuring the difference between the cutterhead body and the cutting edge. After the indicator is set and the magnetic base is on (if available), the indicator point should be pointing straight into the cutterhead. Turn the dial so that it reads zero when the point is resting on the cutterhead body. Rotate the cutterhead until the point of the knife that you are setting gives its highest reading on the dial. If the reading is less than the correct height differential, raise the knife; if it is more, lower the knife. Snug the tightening bolts, paying particular attention to not moving the knife while tightening. After you get one end of the knife exactly right, move the indicator and set the other end. Upon completing that, move the indicator back and recheck the first end to see if it moved while you were adjusting the other end. Recheck and adjust each end and tighten securely.

After all knives have been set correctly, the adjustable outfeed table needs to be set. Set up the indicator as described previously on the non-adjustable outfeed table. Take the zero dial indicator reading and pick up the reading you get when you swing the indicator point over the cutterhead

Determining the distance between the outfeed table and the cutterhead.

and get a reading on the knife point at the top of the cutting circle. The outfeed table is now adjusted so that you get the same zero reading at the top of the cutting circle as on the outfeed table itself.

Bar Magnets and Steel Parallels

Bar magnets and precision-ground steel parallels are used in exactly the same way, the only difference being that magnetism holds the magnets in place a little better so that your hands are free to adjust the knives. For our discussion here I will refer to them both as steel parallels.

Using steel parallels to set knives involves setting the top of the cutting circle perfectly even with the outfeed table. First, the outfeed table is positioned and the steel parallels are set on the outfeed table extending over the top of the cutterhead. Two parallels make the job easier. To obtain the proper knife position, the cutterhead is rotated or "swung" slightly so that the knife being set moves back and forth under the parallel from slightly one side of the apex to the other side and back again. As the cutterhead is oscillating back and forth, the knife is gradually raised until the cutting edge just barely touches or kisses the parallel. Both ends of each knife are set in this manner. The knives are tightened and rechecked for movement. Since the steel parallels are sitting on the outfeed table, the knives are being adjusted so that the top of the cutting circle is in exactly the same plane as the outfeed table. No movement of the outfeed table is necessary — or desirable!

'Crow's Foot' Knife Setting Devices

These knife setting devices are included with some machines as an added bonus but they are not very popular nor are they particularly easy to use. They look like a little three-legged device, or 'crow's foot' with a threaded bolt that screws down between the legs. In use, the knives are set exactly the same as when the dial indicator is used except instead of gauging the knife height to a number, the knives are gauged until they just "kiss" the bolt in the crow's feet. Steel parallels then have to be used to set the outfeed table. The steel parallels are set on the outfeed table as described previously with the outfeed table high enough so that the knife does not touch the parallel as the cutterhead is oscillated to each side of the top of the cutting circle. The table is gradually lowered until the knife just barely kisses the parallel when it is at the apex of its travel. Lock the outfeed table in this position.

Measuring the height of the knives.

Procedure

After you have determined your jointer type, the style of cutterhead, and the device that you are going to use to set the knife height, you can use the following procedure to set your jointer knives:

1. Disconnect power from the machine. An unexpected start while your hands are on the cutterhead is very undesirable. Most jointer cutterheads run about 10,000 surface feet per minute — which translates to 120 miles per hour!

2. Determine the height differential that you want the cutting edge above the cutter body using the information given earlier under *Dial Indicators* or *Steel Parallels*.

3. Remove one knife. See *Cutterheads* section above for procedure. Remember, a knife that is too dull to cut wood efficiently will do a remarkable job at cutting flesh!

4. Clean everything; the dull knife, knife slot, gibbs, screws, and cutterhead. Use steel wool and penetrating oil to remove rust, and use household ammonia to remove pitch and gum. Wipe everything with an oily rag.

5. Insert sharp knife. Adjust the height to the desired cutting circle as described previously. Be sure to recheck the knife after it is securely tightened in case of movement during the tightening.

Now that you have one knife in place, repeat the above procedure until all of your knives have been set.

Next, recheck the knives around the cutterhead in sequence, first doing all knives on one end, then the other end and the middle if you want. If every point of every cutting edge is within .002 or .003 of the desired height, you have done a pretty good job.

After getting all knives in the desired cutting circle, the final adjustment is the outfeed table. Using either a dial indicator or steel parallels, adjust the outfeed table to where the apex of the cutting circle is even (in the same plane as) the surface of the outfeed table. Lock it in place and do not move it until you change knives again or change the cutting circle.

The dull knives should be sent out to be professionally sharpened and match-ground. By keeping your knives match-ground to exactly the same size, your cutterhead will be better balanced and your knives will wear out evenly. The sharpened knives should be protected to prevent nicks and oiled to prevent rust.

Bowed or "bent" knives seem to creep up even in the best of families and come from many different causes. Maybe there was a slight amount of pitch or dirt on the back of the knife or the back of the knife slot when the knife was tightened. Perhaps the knife slot was not perfectly straight when it was made, or maybe the bottom edge of the knife was made with a bow in it. When the knife was sharpened, a bow might have been ground into it, or a bowed knife was clamped flat to be ground and sprung back bowed. About the only thing you can do is to use the knife if the bow isn't intolerable and if it is, throw the knife set away.

It is fairly easy to maintain jointer knife accuracy while in the machine. The most important thing is cleanliness. Do not let sawdust and pitch build up around the knife in use — causing heat, gaulding, and possible misalignment. After a few hours of use on a newly sharpened set of knives, recheck all of the knife heights and, *most importantly*, the outfeed table height.

If all the knives are cutting the same amount, they will also dull evenly. However, if one knife is much duller than the other knives, it is probably cutting more because it is (or was) higher than its co-workers. Rechecking and readjusting can greatly extend the useful life of a set of sharpened knives as well as assuring accuracy.

We have all had the experience of getting a new sharp set of knives adjusted perfectly only to put a great big nick in all three knives by hitting some unseen and devious nail or foreign object. Every piece of wood from then on receives a little bead as a memorial to the "accident." Now that you can set knives accurately, you can recover something from such an unfortunate situation. First, loosen one knife, slide it 1/8 inch to the right and retighten it in the same cutting circle. Next, do the same for the next knife, only slide it 1/8 inch to the left. Leave the third knife alone. Now you still have nicks in your knives but they do not line up. Wherever one knife has a nick, two others have a good cutting edge! The ends will no longer be matched for rabbeting and you are limited to going through the above procedure to just a couple of times, but you still can get some use out of sharpened knives that you would previously consider ruined.

To keep your jointer tables shiny and new-looking and to prevent rust, particularly in humid weather, **do not** wipe the tables with silicone, graphite, oils, or waxes. Each of these substances will rub off of the table and into the wood as it slides along the tables, preventing the finishing materials from penetrating the pores of the wood. The only thing that has been known to work without adversely affecting subsequent finishing operations is talcum bath powder. It is easy to apply with a blackboard eraser and if done weekly during humid weather, machined surfaces should not be harmed by moisture in the air.

In closing, remember that setting jointer knives requires a good measure of care and patience, and with some experience, you may get so good at it that you enjoy it. And most of all, please be very, very careful.

Using bar magnets or steel parallels to set the height of the knives.

ABOUT THE AUTHOR:
Thomas W. Miller is a woodworker living in Winchester, Virginia.

Jointer Knife Setting Gauge

AN INEXPENSIVE TOOL YOU CAN MAKE YOURSELF

By Roger Sherman

How accurate is accurate? How close is close enough?
Only the individual craftsman knows the answer, because only he knows how he will compensate for the difference.

There is one tool which has no readily available method to compensate for a mis-adjusted cutting edge — the jointer. On the jointer, the knife's edge is either in the same plane as the outfeed table's surface or the stock being run through is ruined. Ruined in that a wedge is developed or a cup at the end (snipe) is formed — either way, you have problems which you do not need.

The knife setting gauge shown can help eliminate the problem of setting the knives correctly. It can be made from odds and ends around the shop and its accuracy — given careful workmanship — is within ± .075 mm.

There are a number of critical areas in making the gauge; namely, no slop in the two pivots, in the cylinder between the wall and the piston, the distance between the front feet and the center of the piston's foot, the registration arm's length and the gauge's weight.

I made the gauge from 5/16'' pieces of mahogany but I found out that this made the device too light. The weight of the registration arm at 10'' and the force generated by the jointer's adjusting screw in raising the knife against the piston lifted the gauge off the outfeed table. Therefore, use thicker sections or use 5/16'' but lay a heavy "C" clamp on top of the gauge when you use it. Also, use dimensionally stable wood.

The first thing to do is determine how much of an 'arc' you want to see on the scale; i.e., how much of an up or down movement of the jointer's knife do you want to see recorded? Realistically, you should be able to set the knives by eye and a steel ruler or piece of wood to within 1/32'' of the final height. The recording on the scale depends on the registration arm's length. The arm's length determines the length of the gauge.

The formula is as follows:
Da - Distance the piston moves up or down.
Ds - Distance shown on the scale.
Ls - Length of the registration arm.
Lp - Length of the piston.

$$\frac{Da \quad x \quad Ls}{Lp} = Ds$$

Let's substitute a few numbers to see how the formula works. Let us say that you have to move the blade of the jointer up 1/32'' to have it even with the outfeed table. Let us also say you want a 10'' registration arm and a 1 ¾'' piston length. How much of an 'arc' will the movement of the knife record if it is moved 1/32''? For simplicity, convert the fractions to decimals.

Da - 1/32 - .03123
Ls - 10 - 10.0
Lp - 1 ¾ - 1.75

$$\frac{.03123 \times 10.0}{1.75} = .17857 - 3/16''$$

Thus, if the knife's edge is moved 1/32'', up or down, on a 10'' registration arm, with a 1 ¾'' piston arm, the distance recorded will be a total of 3/8'' — that is, 3/16'' up and 3/16'' down.

After you have determined how long you want the arm, add about three inches to take into account the thickness of the gauge's end caps, scale width and movement space.

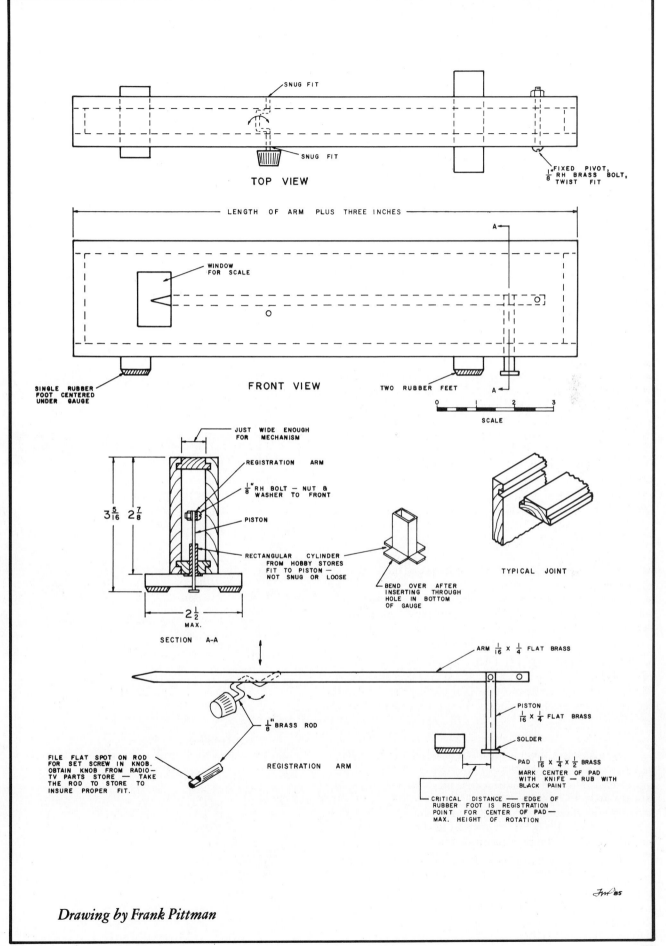

SNUG FIT

SNUG FIT

TOP VIEW

FIXED PIVOT, $\frac{1}{8}$" RH BRASS BOLT, TWIST FIT

LENGTH OF ARM PLUS THREE INCHES

A

WINDOW FOR SCALE

A

FRONT VIEW

SINGLE RUBBER FOOT CENTERED UNDER GAUGE

TWO RUBBER FEET

SCALE

JUST WIDE ENOUGH FOR MECHANISM

REGISTRATION ARM

$\frac{1}{8}$" RH BOLT — NUT & WASHER TO FRONT

PISTON

RECTANGULAR CYLINDER FROM HOBBY STORES FIT TO PISTON — NOT SNUG OR LOOSE

$3\frac{5}{16}$ $2\frac{7}{8}$

$2\frac{1}{2}$ MAX.

SECTION A-A

BEND OVER AFTER INSERTING THROUGH HOLE IN BOTTOM OF GAUGE

TYPICAL JOINT

ARM $\frac{1}{16}$ X $\frac{1}{4}$ FLAT BRASS

$\frac{1}{8}$" BRASS ROD

PISTON $\frac{1}{16}$ X $\frac{1}{4}$ FLAT BRASS

SOLDER

FILE FLAT SPOT ON ROD FOR SET SCREW IN KNOB. OBTAIN KNOB FROM RADIO-TV PARTS STORE — TAKE THE ROD TO STORE TO INSURE PROPER FIT.

REGISTRATION ARM

PAD $\frac{1}{16}$ X $\frac{1}{4}$ X $\frac{1}{2}$ BRASS MARK CENTER OF PAD WITH KNIFE — RUB WITH BLACK PAINT

CRITICAL DISTANCE — EDGE OF RUBBER FOOT IS REGISTRATION POINT FOR CENTER OF PAD — MAX. HEIGHT OF ROTATION

Drawing by Frank Pittman

Make the brass pieces first. They can be obtained from a hobby store. Mark the holes for the pivots, punch and drill with a **sharp** 1/8'' metal twist drill. Remember — no slop! Next, cut the rectangular cylinder to size allowing about ¼'' to extend pass the bottom of the floor piece. Cut through the corners of the rectangular piece to a depth of ¼''. The flaps will be bent over once the cylinder is inserted into a hole cut into the floor piece of the gauge. These flaps are epoxied to the floor piece. Next, scribe a line down the center of the piston's length and also widthwise across the foot. These two lines should coincide when assembled. Solder the foot to the piston. On the edge of the foot, cut a line with a knife which coincides with the one scribed across the width. Put some type of light paint in this cut so that it is easily seen.

Put a point on the registration arm's end which will be on the scale and cut the scale to length. An old steel ruler will do fine. The "U" shaped rod has to wait until you make the sides of the gauge. The bends have to be within the enclosure but can rub on the sides.

To use the gauge, place it on the outfeed table and by means of the knob on the "U" rod, lower the foot to the table. There should be no movement due to slop in the piston's arm where it attaches to the registration arm or where the registration attaches to the fixed pivot. If there is movement, put a piece of paper under the foot to see if that cancels it out. You may have to use a little "Kentucky Windage" here and there to cancel out the slop. However, there is just so much you can do to correct inaccurate workmanship, dull tools, and carelessness before the accuracy of the device is lost.

Once the foot is on the table and the slop, if any, is gone, mark the scale at the zero point shown by the arm's point. From this mark, paint an area 3/16'' above and below. If the pointer falls into the area below the zero point, the jointer blade is above the outfeed table: above means below.

Next, move the gauge so that the front edges of both rubber feet are on the edge of the outfeed table. The line which you cut into the foot of the piston should now be over the knife's edge at the highest point on its rotation. Move the knife up or down to zero on the scale. Do this across the table at the middle and the other end. Check once again to see that the knife is in plane across its length. Tighten the knife into position and move to the next knife. Remember, the knife's tightening screw, if right hand threaded, will tend to move the knife upward — just enough to be a breath out of plane. You may want to compensate for the tendency.

To test the setting, set a piece of wood on the outfeed table but overhanging the knives. Rotate the knives by hand. There should be a whisper on the piece of wood as each knife moves pass. If the knife catches, readjust, remembering to zero first.

The gauge is accurate to a reasonable degree. It is not absolutely precise to a thousandth of an inch but it is as accurate as the materials and workmanship allow. I have used the gauge for a year now and have had no problems. Anything run through the jointer comes out flat and true. Since my outfeed table is aluminum, a magnet would not help if it were put on the feet — however, if your outfeed table is steel, the magnets will be better than the rubber feet.

If your jointer has a moveable outfeed table, the procedure is the same. The key is that the knife must be in plane with the outfeed table. Do the best you can and if you do, the gauge will turn out to be accurate, cost effective and a time saving device.

ABOUT THE AUTHOR

Roger Sherman is a woodworker living in Baltimore, Maryland.

A Pusher for the Jointer

For table-saw work, the simplest of push sticks — a foot-long scrap of 1 × 2 with a V-notch in one end, for example — is suitable. But pushing work over a jointer's cutterhead calls for something a little more sophisticated.

The jointer is considered by many woodworkers to be the most dangerous power tool in the shop. Edge jointing can be done safely enough using your hands to hold and push the work piece, but surfacing the face of a board is a different matter. In this process, there is no safe way — using just your hands — to hold the work piece firmly against the table and push it over the cutterhead. The danger is obvious: There's but a fraction of an inch of wood between your hand and the cutterhead.

The shop-built pusher shown here is just the ticket for safe and effective surface jointing. It helps hold the work piece flat on the jointer table, while at the same time allowing the woodworker to push it over the cutterhead safely.

The pusher is made of three scraps of hardwood. The sole is ¾'' × 3'' × 8''. The heel is ¼'' × ¾'' × 3'' and is glued in place. The handle is shaped from a piece ¾'' × 6'' × 8''. Miter two corners to shape the piece, then lay out and cut the grip. Drill 1''-diameter holds at each end of the grip and use a saber saw to saw out the waste between the holes. Ease the exposed edges of the handle using a ¼'' rounding-over bit in a router. Glue the handle to the sole.

A longer, wider pusher can be made using the same general design. On the longer pusher, leave the corners of the handle square and cut a long grip parallel to the sole. Then you can grasp the pusher with both hands when jointing a long work piece.

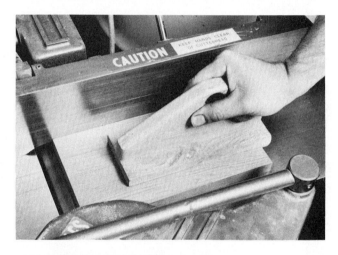

The Answer: Shapers

Editor's note: *The following discussion of shapers is from "The Answer," a column by Ernie Conover that appeared regularly in* American Woodworker.

The shaper is one of the least understood tools in the shop, and yet it is the real workhorse of any woodworking firm, be it small shop or huge factory. The shaper is also right up there with the jointer on the danger list. In fact, I think most would-be users are quite intimidated by the machine, and rightfully so.

Making matters worse, there is not much written about the use of the shaper. There is a nice booklet, originally published in the 1930s by the Rockwell-Delta folks, which is now being republished by Sterling. Unfortunately, this book is meant for the Delta home shop shaper, which is very small by industrial standards, and practices are outlined that are questionable by today's standards. Furthermore, the book must be applied very selectively to larger shapers.

Although the router came after the shaper, it is a tool so familiar to everyone that I will use it to help conceptualize the shaper. In principle, the shaper is a router and router table. It consists of a table (usually of cast iron) with a hole in the middle for the arbor and one or two slots running across it for a miter gauge. Shaper bases vary from simple stamped steel stands (such as in the Delta design) to total enclosures of cast iron or sheet metal. Mounted to the top of the table is the fence, which guides the work past the cutter. Mounted under the table is a motor and the arbor. Now, let's look at each of the components in detail.

TABLES

Although most shaper tables are made of cast iron, there is no reason why sheet steel or even wood wouldn't be perfectly usable. Whatever it is made of, the main things to look for in a table are flatness and size. But don't get carried away with flatness, as the table needs to be flat only to about $1/64$ inch. In fact, the flatness of a sheet of medium density fiber board would serve nicely. Within reason, a shaper table can't be too big, especially in width. Obviously, the table shouldn't be deeper than an easy reach of any operator, but plenty of width to support long work promotes safety and chatter-free cuts. I have always wondered why manufacturers don't offer L-shaped extension wings that bolt to the table sides. This would really make running long moldings a joy.

In the marketplace, tables seem to range from about 15 inches square for very light duty models to about 30 by 40 inches for industrial monsters. Table height seems to vary quite a bit too, but 30 to 35 inches from the floor seems right for most people.

STANDS

Most shapers come with a stand. I know of no tabletop models on the market; the height and accessibility would not be correct. Enclosed cabinet-type stands are safer, and one with an inside compartment makes a nice dust-free environment for your cutters, providing you remember to close the door. In addition to these points, the stand should be solid and stable.

FENCES

When buying a shaper, it's extremely important to get a good fence. Good fence design promotes high-grade work with ease and safety. Things to look for in the hypothetical perfect fence (does one exist?) are rigidity, size, ease of adjustment, chip ejection, dust collection, and guarding. Above all, a fence must be rigid, because any movement from a flimsy design will show up as chatter in the work. Cast iron with wood facing seems to be the material of choice, but there is no reason that steel fabrications wouldn't work just as well. A fence has to be big enough to support work adequately, but this is relative to the size of the shaper. Above all, avoid fences that are too low. Plenty of height is nice to support such things as panel doors while using a vertical panel-raising cutter. Often this problem can be overcome by substituting wider wood facing.

Adjustments should be easy and positive. The two halves of the fence should adjust in relation to one another, and the entire fence should move in relation to the cutter. On most shapers, the latter is accomplished by loosening the bolts that hold the fence to the table and gently persuading the fence with a heavy object. I have always called this "nudge adjustment."

Finally, the two halves of the fence should open and close.

GUARDS

Good guarding can't be over-emphasized. Additionally, it's imperative to have some type of hold-down mechanism that keeps wood firmly in place and keeps fingers away from the cutter.

Often, locally fabricated feather boards or an investment in one of the good after-market systems such as Shop Guide will accomplish this.

Last but not least, there should be good dust pick-up provided.

SPINDLES

Common spindle sizes are ½, ¾, 1, and 1¼ inches. Home shop shapers are pretty much limited to ½-inch spindles, because this is all amateurs and most small cabinet shops need. With today's move toward bigger cutters, however, larger spindles probably are in order. If you plan to run the traditional three-wing HSS cutter no larger than 2½ inches in diameter, a ½-inch spindle will do fine. If you plan to run today's larger carbide cutters, especially stacked cutters such as panel door sets, then a ¾-inch spindle is a good idea. For true industrial use, such as running 6-inch and larger horizontal panel-raising cutters, 1 or 1¼ inches is a must.

The best of all worlds is one of the new cartridge-type spindles. The spindle is mounted in the quill via a keyed taper so that various sizes can be substituted at will. This allows the user to use an entire range of cutters safely.

Historically, a shaper spindle was turned counterclockwise, and work was fed from the righthand side of the machine (into the cutter). By employing a reversing motor to give clockwise rotation, all cutters can do double duty by being turned upside down and feeding work from the left side. Most modern shapers have this feature, but some system must be employed to prevent the spindle nut (holding the cutter stack) from unscrewing during clockwise rotation. A minimum of a keyed washer under the nut (such as in the Delta design), and preferably double nuts, is necessary.

Once, spindle speed was 9,500 rotations per minute—and that was it. With the modern move to larger cutters, shaper manufacturers have added multiple speeds to their machines. This makes sense. It is nice to have three stepped speeds, with the top speed being 9,500 rpm. With the added speed comes added danger. Just as when mounting large work in a lathe, if you mount large cutters, you must remember to switch to low speed and increase it with caution.

One of the most important features to look at in spindle design is how it is raised and lowered. Frequent height adjustments are required, so it should be easy, safe, and should lock positively once set. An adjustment that drifts can have disastrous consequences when a $450 carbide cutter head inbeds itself in the table.

MOTORS

Finally, we come to the motor, and there is not much to say. For small ½-inch spindles, ½ or ¾ horsepower is adequate. For larger shapers, 2 to 5 horsepower is in order. Just as important as the motor is the method of power transmission. Some larger machines have direct drive, which has the virtue of being positive. Mostly, power is transmitted by belts, however. Because the quill must move up and down, a flat-belt drive often is employed. Be sure that it is positive.

In summary, the reader will appreciate that buying a shaper is a lot more complicated than meets the eye. Also, if one has never used a shaper before, the author would strongly recommend spending some time with someone who is experienced. This may be a hard person to find. The average industrial arts teacher may not know a lot more than is in the above-mentioned old Rockwell-Delta book.

Look very carefully at the type of cutter you will be using. For instance, I have talked to a lot of disgruntled owners of Sears shapers who found that the opening in the fence is not large enough to handle stacked cabinet door sets.

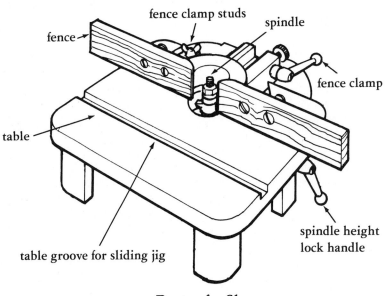

Parts of a Shaper

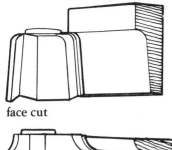
face cut

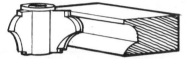
¼-inch and ½-inch
quarter round

¾-inch quarter round

½-inch cove and ⁵⁄₁₆-inch
quarter round

⅛-inch and ⅜-inch quarter round
and ¼-inch bead

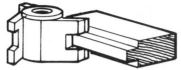
wedge tongue

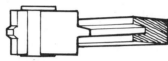
wedge groove

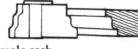
female sash

male sash

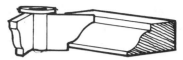
ogee

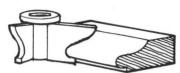
bead table edge

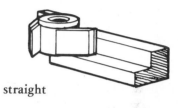
straight

Some Common Shaper Cutter Profiles

Shaper cutters are larger and come in a greater variety of profiles than router bits. Passes with two different router bits would be required to cut the edge shape being machined here in a single pass.

The Answer: Plate Joinery

Editor's note: *The following discussion of plate joinery is from "The Answer," a column by Ernie Conover that appeared regularly in* American Woodworker.

Plate joining is a flexible, fast, and super-strong alternative to dowel joints or the more time-consuming mortise and tenon joint. The idea was conceived in the 1950s by Swiss woodworker Herman Steiner, who was dissatisfied with the dowel joint. As we all are painfully aware, dowel joints have to be perfect in two axes to get a perfect alignment, and few if any dowel jigs do the job consistently. By using a saw blade 4 inches in diameter to cut a 1/52-inch-wide circular kerf that accepts a small, elliptical wood plate, Steiner created a joint that was always in alignment in one axis and had 1/8 inch of latitude in the other. The crux of his invention was the biscuits that were made from compressed beech wood. Any water-base glue makes the plate expand and hold fast.

Although Steiner perfected his idea using a table saw to cut the joints, his real contribution was in developing a portable machine to do the job in foolproof fashion.

The fruition of Steiner's work is Steiner Lamello AG in Bubendorf, Switzerland, which manufactures his gadget and distributes it worldwide. Steiner's patents now have run out and others are making such equipment, but the name Lamello is synonymous with plate joinery the way Kleenex is with facial tissue.

Since Lamello was first, we should discuss that company's two machines first. Elu, a German firm, makes a machine that is innovative, but no longer seems to market it. Virutex, a Spanish company, markets a machine that is a cross-breed of the two Lamello models.

PLATES

Plates, whether they come from Lamello, Elu, or Virutex, seem pretty much the same. At least I have not been able to find any difference in fit or strength. Lamello calls them plates, Elu calls them biscuits, and Virutex calls them tablets; all these terms are descriptive. Biscuit is particularly good because I was able to pawn a couple off on my kids as treats. (High in fiber but hard on the teeth.) They are all made from beech and are compressed with a waffle pattern on them. The grain runs diagonally across the plate, giving maximum strength to the joint. Plates come in three sizes, but all are the same thickness and have edges which are arcs of the same circle. The smallest, No. 0, is 2.2 by 3 inches, while the No. 10 is 2.4 by 4 inches and the No. 20 is 2.6 by 5 inches. Within 10 minutes of assembly, the plate swells up and clamps can be removed. In fact, disassembly for a goof often means damaging the work even though the glue is not dry.

CUTTERS

The best machine that Lamello makes is the Top. All other machines use the same principles as the Top to get the job done. The Top has a swinging fence that allows the slot to be aligned in reference to the face of the work. This is one of the great advantages of biscuit joinery; the face always comes out in perfect registration. Plate size is set by a convenient cam at the right side of the base. The fence is used at right angles for things like face frames. The fence can be swung straight up and the bench top used to register the work face. Finally, the fence can be set to any angle joint work at angles other than 45 or 90 degrees. This is the one thing the Top can do that the other machines can't, but how often special angles are necessary only the reader can decide. Also, special jigs can be made up for the other machines for the "once in a while" job.

In using the Top extensively there is one other advantage that would make me pick it as a commercial user, but that I could live without as an amateur. That is the fact that when the fence is used at right angles, it consistently places the cut the same distance from the edge and in at a perfect distance for 3/4-inch or 1-inch material. By adding a small clip-on shim to the fence, the machine is right for 1/2-inch material. This means that a piece made this week will interchange with a piece made last year. This is an important benefit for production work, but unimportant for builders of one-of-a-kind pieces.

The Top is packed in a very nice wood box with an array of accessories and tools. The box is plate-jointed together, but my one criticism of it is that there is no way to keep the sliding door to the tool compartment closed, and I had to add a wood toggle. Made entirely of cast aluminum, the Top also is the most powerful machine on the market, with a 600-watt motor driving the blade at 8,000 rpm. It also has a slip clutch that prevents overloading the motor if the operator plunges the cut too fast. At the rather hefty price of $580, the two advantages (angle joints and consistent registration) have to be weighed.

The second plate-joining machine in the Lamello line is the Junior. My guess is that it is an attempt by Lamello to bring a lower-priced machine to the amateur and small-shop market. It is much cheaper at a price of $385. The fence on the Junior is a separate piece that attaches via two clamps. It is up to the user to adjust the fence for the right amount of off-set for the job. The fence can be reversed for 45-degree work. The Junior we had for testing was of molded plastic construction, but the importer, Colonial Saw Company, informed us that as of the next batch it will have a cast aluminum base. The Junior is less powerful, with a 500-watt motor turning at 10,000 rpm, and no slip clutch to prevent overload. I liked the Junior save one thing: The mechanism for changing plate size is crude. Instead of a simple cam, the machine is set to No. 20 plates, and spring clips must be inserted on the camshaft to use No. 0 and No. 10

Here's a roundup of the plate-joining machines on the market. Left, front to back: Lamello Top, Freud JS100, Virutex 0-81, Elu 3380. Right, front to back: Kaiser Mini 3-D, Lamello Standard, Lamello Junior, Porter-Cable 555.

plates. This is inconvenient, and the clips get lost in sawdust easily. Also, the Junior is simply packed in a cardboard box so there is no place to store the clips and accessories.

Speaking of sawdust, plate joiners make a lot of it. Lamello has a nifty vacuum hose attachment that makes the machine very clean to operate. In view of the fact that one joint really messes up a shop, the extra cost is justified if you like things clean and neat or do a lot of on-site installations.

The Elu Machine is very well made, but is really a groove-cutting machine, with a pivoting head that allows it to cut biscuit joints as well. Since it isn't clear whether the Elu is any longer marketed it is not covered here other than to say that it does give acceptable performance.

The Virutex basically is a copy of the Junior, right down to the scales on the front of the base, but with some improvements. It is entirely made of cast aluminum, with

little plastic other than in knobs and the motor housing. Virutex also dispensed with the spring clip adjustment for tablet size and used a cam like the Lamello Top. The Virutex is quite powerful, with a 550-watt motor turning the cutter at 10,000 rpm, but has no slip clutch. The machine is nicely packaged in a plastic carrying case, which has storage compartments for all of the accessories and a few tablets. At an average price of $325, it is a good buy.

Both Lamello and Virutex make a variety of special hinges and fasteners that can be installed with the joining machine. Lamello's Paumelle hinges are very nice for both flush-face and overlay door installations. A single stroke of the joining machine inlets both the door and the frame. Paumelle hinges come in nickel, brass, and black. For those needing a knock-down application, Lamello makes two types and Virutex makes one. They all seem good, but Virutex seems the best value.

BLADES

The blades in all of the machines are carbide-tipped and can be sharpened by a good saw service. Colonial Saw told me that a blade is good for about 40,000 penetrations in particleboard and many more in hardwood. The Junior does not have the same blade as the Top, but those ordering a replacement get a Top blade, which is about $85. Plates, biscuits, or tablets seem to run about $28 per 1,000, regardless of size. That makes them cheap, but they go fast. I counted 110 biscuits in a kitchen cabinet I made recently. Also, they must be kept dry, so a sealed plastic container is in order. If they get wet, they swell up by about 50 percent and are ruined.

One thing worth mentioning is that plate joinery is really strong in particleboard and plywood—stronger than any other method I have found. With the increased use of these materials, I am sure many people will turn to biscuits.

It is very easy to build boxes with biscuit joinery whether they are made of plywood or hardwood. It does take clamping in four directions for 10 minutes. Lamello makes a band clamp for this purpose, but it is only good for large boxes or frames. If you like quick, trouble-free joinery that stays together, then consider plates.

Cutting a biscuit joint is fast and easy. 1. Decide where the biscuits should be located, then mark their positions on the face of the board.

2. Set the plate joiner fence to center the groove on the edge of the board.

3. Line up the machine with the pencil marks, and cut the grooves.

4. Apply glue to the biscuits and the edges of the pieces to be joined, insert the biscuits, and assemble the joint.

Commonsense Tool Maintenance

By Gene and Katie Hamilton

With a little know-how and some simple maintenance techniques you can make your power tools top performers.

SHARPNESS COUNTS

The easiest step you can take to prolong the life of your tools is to always use sharp blades, bits and other accessories. For example, many failures with circular saws are due to a dull blade. A person will buy a saw, put it to work and continue to use it after the blade is worn. You can overheat and damage the saw motor every time you use it with a dull blade. Sharpening the blade or buying a new one costs only a fraction of the price of a new saw.

Fit the tool to the job and avoid forcing a tool to do more than it is designed to handle. This will also help keep your tool from overheating. You can prevent overheating by using commonsense. When your tool gets too uncomfortable to hold, stop cutting or drilling. Let it run without load for a few seconds. It will cool down faster running free than if you turn it off and set it down. Be careful when cooling a tool in this manner; that spinning blade or drill is dangerous and can cause serious injury.

Choose an appropriate extension cord for your tools. A common cause of overheated and burned out tools is undersized extension cords. Generally for a 3/8-in. drill, a standard 18-gauge heavy-duty cord is good for at least 50 ft. If you use a cord over 50 ft. long, especially with a circular saw, consult the table or your tool manual for proper wire gauge.

CLEAN AND WELL LUBRICATED

Keeping your tools clean is the next step. A clean tool runs cool. Sawdust and dirt buildup inside the tool can combine with moisture, wood resins, and oil to form a solid mass that can block the air flow and the design of the insulation.

A good rule of thumb is to clean your tools after every ten hours of use. Keep the cord and body of the tool clean according to the manufacturer's recommendations. Be careful in selecting a cleaning solution. Don't use one that contains carbon tetrachloride, chlorinated cleaning solvents or ammonia because they'll damage the plastic housing. Don't store tools in direct sunlight which damages the plastic and rubber parts of tools.

Vacuum the dirt and dust out from inside your tools or blow the tool clean with compressed air. One easy way is to place the hose in the exhaust end of a shop vac and turn the air on the tool while it is running. Direct the air through the intake ports using the tool's air flow to help.

Many popular-priced tools have sleeve bearings that should be oiled every ten hours. For example, on most popular priced sanders, there's an oil reservoir, a felt pad that holds oil and secretes it to the bearing as it gets warm. The pad holds only about ten drops, so avoid over oiling. Excess oil will run inside the tool and cause problems.

Many of the popular priced tools have brush systems that are designed to last the useful life of the tool. If you take care of your tool or purchase heavy duty tools sooner or later you will have to replace the motor brushes. Many owner's manuals do not give instructions for replacing the brushes because manufacturers are designing consumer tools today to meet strict safety regulations with double insulation. Replacing the brushes incorrectly or with the wrong part will defeat

After every 10 hours blow out the accumulated dust and dirt by directing a stream of air into the air intake port as the tool is run.

the double insulated safety feature. If you have a tool that does not have brushes that are under easy to remove covers you are probably better off taking the tool in for service when the brushes need work.

If your tool stops, and you suspect the brushes are at fault, try this trick: Tap the top of the housing to see if you can free the brush. If it is hung up in its channel, this will work. If it doesn't work, the brushes probably are worn and have to be replaced.

RECHARGEABLES

Using a rechargeable tool is the best way to keep it running well. Keep it fully charged, always recharging it before you use it or before you put it away.

If it doesn't seem to hold a charge like it did when new, it might be suffering from 'nicad memory'. This forms in the battery if the tool is discharged to about the same point every time it is used. To help eliminate this, discharge the batteries completely and then fully recharge them, completing this cycle several times. This will help restore full capacity to a battery that may seem faulty. Keep the battery fully charged and stored out of temperature extremes for maximum use.

Keep the plunger arm of the saber saw clean and well lubricated. Wipe with an oily rag occasionally.

Most consumer grade tools have sleeve bearings at the end of the armature. Oil felt pad lightly every 10 hours with #20 oil.

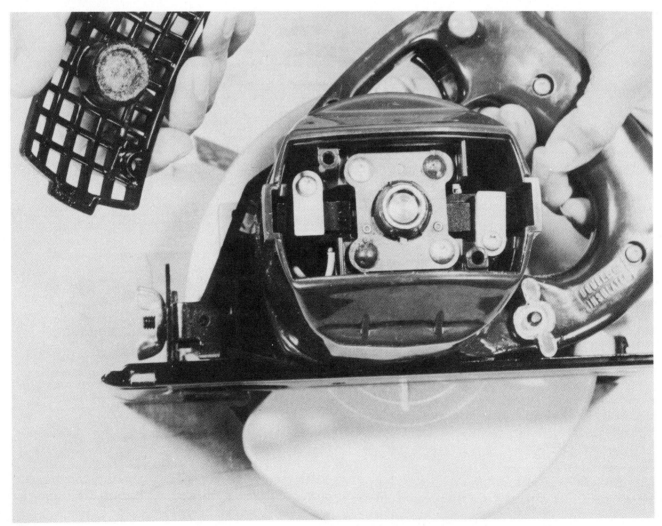

60

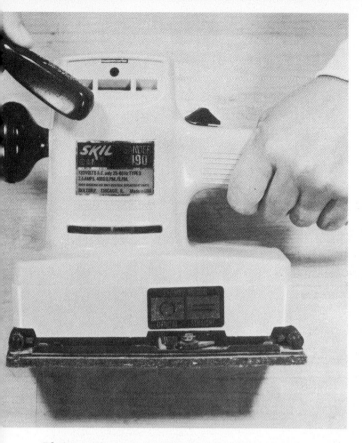

If the tool stops or runs rough, the brushes may be hung up. Before replacing, tap the housing at the opposite end from the fan to free the brushes.

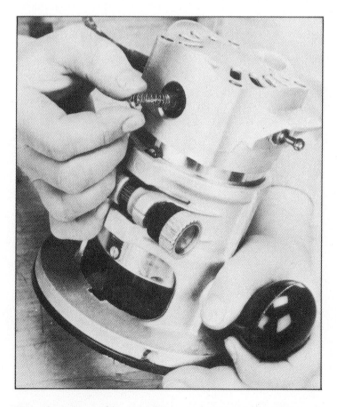

Most brushes of heavy duty tools are easily replaced if they are located at the end of the armature opposite the fan.

MAINTENANCE SCHEDULE

DRILL
1. Use sharp drills and accessories
2. Don't overload tool
3. Use recommended extension cord
4. Keep tool and cord clean (avoid strong solvents)
5. Store out of direct sunlight
6. Oil bearing at end of armature after 10 hours of operation (Unplug tool for all maintenance)
7. Blow out tool after 20-25 hours of operation (Unplug tool for all maintenance)
8. Check brush wear
9. Repack gear case with approved lubricant

SANDERS
1. Change sandpaper often
2. Do not force tool
3. Use recommended extension cord
4. Keep tool and cord clean (avoid strong solvents)
5. Store out of direct sunlight
6. Oil bearing at top of armature opposite fan after 10 hours of operation (Unplug tool for all maintenance)
7. Blow out tool after 20-25 hours of operation (Unplug tool for all maintenance)
8. Check brush wear

BELT SANDERS
1. Change sanding belt often, as needed
2. Do not force tool
3. Use recommended extension cord
4. Keep tool and cord clean (avoid strong solvents)
5. Store out of direct sunlight
6. Oil bearing lightly in front pulley (some belt sanders have sealed bearings on front pulley) after 10 hours of operation (Unplug tool for all maintenance)
7. Blow out tool after 20-25 hours of operation (Unplug tool for all maintenance)
8. Inspect drive belt if so equipped
9. Check brush wear

SABER SAW
1. Change blade when dull
2. Do not force tool
3. Use recommended extension cord
4. Keep tool and cord clean (avoid strong solvents)
5. Store out of direct sunlight
6. Oil bearing at end of armature opposite fan after 10 hours of operation (Unplug tool for all maintenance)
7. Blow out tool after 20-25 hours of operation (Unplug tool for all maintenance)
8. Clean and oil plunger arm (arm that holds blade)
9. Check brush wear
10. Repack gear case with approved lubricant

CIRCULAR SAW
1. Change blade often
2. Do not force tool
3. Use recommended extension cord
4. Keep tool and cord clean (avoid strong solvents)
5. Store out of direct sunlight
6. Oil bearing at end of armature opposite fan after 10 hours of operation (Unplug tool for all maintenance)
7. Blow out tool and clear air outlet by blade after 20-25 hours of operation (Unplug tool for all maintenance)
8. Remove blade, clean out and inspect blade guard (guard should snap and remain closed when saw is held inverted)
9. Check brush wear
10. Repack gear case with approved lubricant

Most belt sanders have a sleeve bearing on the front idler pulley. Oil it lightly after 10 hours of operation.

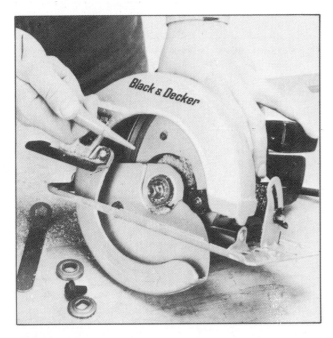

Change the blade often on a circular saw. When the blade is off, clean the blade guard and see that it snaps shut and remains there when the saw is inverted. Oil lightly if it binds.

RECOMMENDED EXTENSION CORDS
Wire Gauge Chart A.W.G.

NOTE: The smaller the gauge number, the heavier the wire. The bold type gauge numbers are extra heavy duty cords.

Name Plate Amps.	25 ft. to 50 ft.	51 ft. to 100 ft.	101 ft. to 200 ft.
0-2	18	18	18
2-3	18	18	**16**
3-4	18	18	**16**
4-5	18	18	**14**
5-6	18	16	**14**
6-8	18	16	**12**
8-10	18	14	**12**
10-12	**16**	14	**10**
12-14	**16**	12	**10**

Using The Dial Indicator In The Woodworking Shop

by Thomas W. Miller

FIG. 4: *Indicating blade flange runout. Notice that the base is resting on the wooden table and the magnetic base is 'off'.*

Does your radial arm saw always seem to splinter one side of the wood or the other?

Does your band saw vibrate excessively and you just can't seem to figure out why?

Does your table saw fence always seem to be pinching or skewed away from the blade?

If so, then maybe this article will help to lead you to a solution to these problems and others.

The magnetic base dial indicator is probably the handiest device to have around when you are setting up or aligning practically any machine in the workshop. Yet very few shops have one, and even fewer woodworkers know of its many uses. Not only is the quality of the cuts substantially better, but the safety and ease of use are noticeably improved.

I always enjoy going into a man's shop about three months after he has purchased and started using a dial indicator. He always is startled at all the difference that it has made, and usually I hear a twenty minute testimonial of its benefits—complete with examples and samples of proof! In just three months he has become such a believer that he would rather give up his steel tape measure than his dial indicator.

The dial indicator is available on the market in an infinite number of variations, most of which are designed for the metal-working industry and are not very usable in woodworking applications. Most all dial indicator assemblies consist of the dial indicator, connecting arm, one or two double knuckles, and a base. The best bases have an enclosed permanent magnet with an on / off switch. The on / off switch has nothing to do with electricity; it merely slides the internal magnetic poles between an aligned / misaligned position.

63

FIG. 1: *Indicating T-Slot parallel to blade. Notice how the indicator base is clamped to the miter gauge—the magnetic base is 'off'.*

This causes the base to be either a very strong magnet or no magnet at all! The arm and knuckles enable you to position the point of the indicator in just about any angle, in any plane that you want.

A word of warning: The knuckle assemblies are so double-jointed that most first-time users find it difficult to get the indicator positioned just right. Don't get too frustrated; you'll get better at it with a little practice and even very experienced users have to wrestle with it from time to time.

The magnetic-base dial indicator can be used in any position on any machine in the woodworking shop. It will align a fence, check blade or pulley run-out, set cutterhead knives, and even measure veneer or other inlay materials.

Not only will it do so many things, it will do them with incredible accuracy. The indicator dial is graduated in .001″ and is accurate and repeatable throughout the entire range. (Usually one inch total travel). Therefore, the woodworker who is very meticulous in setting up his machines and always gets them within 1/64″ (.015″) will find the improvement phenomenal when he achieves accuracy of .001″ with the dial indicator. His regular cuts will not only be cleaner and smoother, but he will be able to make compound cuts and work with veneers that he would never have attempted before.

An average, or even marginal, machine that is aligned perfectly accurately will completely out-perform a much better machine that is aligned and set up about average. So, an investment of about $75 to $100 will have the effect of upgrading every stationary machine in the shop, thus saving the expense and trouble of machine replacement.

There are two main areas where the dial indicator proves itself indispensable to the woodworker. The first is alignment and setting up the components of a machine accurately. This may be assembling a new machine, rebuilding or repairing a machine, or simply periodic realigning the fence, arm, blade, etc. to maintain acceptable accuracy.

The second situation occurs when trouble arises and you don't know the cause. The dial indicator enables you to go over the machine, one part at a time, and either find the problem or eliminate each part as a suspect. Thus, it becomes rather simple to find the problem without having to disassemble a lot of unnecessary components.

Use

In use, the dial reading on the indicator merely gives you a numerical reading in one-thousandths of an inch—.001″. Each individual indicator reading can be compared to other measurements or to a constant. It will also display numerically gradual deviations from a constant or norm.

In practical terms, it is a rather simple device to use. The base is either attached magnetically to any ferrous metal surface adjacent to the area being indicated, or it may be clamped with a C-clamp, or just left on a flat surface and held in place by gravity. The knuckles and shaft are then adjusted and tightened down so that the indicator point is touching and perpendicular to the surface being indicated. The dial of the indicator may be adjusted to zero or any other convenient starting point.

You will notice that the end of the indicator shaft opposite the point can be lifted to raise the spring-loaded indicator point. It is recommended that the point be lifted in this manner between points of measurement when the indicator point would be rubbing along a rough surface or up against a shoulder that might damage the indicator shaft.

We shall now look into some of the very useful applications of the dial indicator on each individual woodworking machine. For a complete description of jointer applications, see the chapter "Setting Jointer Knives," on page 46.

Table Saw

Practically every table saw is misaligned more than owners want to admit. The blade, arbor, flanges, and bearings can be checked as described in the radial arm saw section.

On the table saw, the arbor is the only thing that can't be adjusted, so you adjust everything to the arbor. First, the T-slot must be square with the arbor or parallel to the side of the blade. To check out this adjustment, the indicator base is clamped with a C-clamp to the miter gauge. *(See Fig. 1)* It is not important what angle is on the miter gauge; you can set it at 45º, and it will still work just as well. With the base clamped to the miter gauge, leave the magnet off and slide the miter gauge and base in the T-slot back and forth beside the blade to make sure that it slides smoothly; if it doesn't, clean everything up until it glides easily.

FIG. 2: *Indicating the Table Saw Fence parallel to the blade. The point must be as low on the blade as possible and the indicator stem should be nearly perpendicular to the blade.*

FIG. 3: *Aligning the fence splitter on the table saw.*

Mount a decent quality blade of the largest diameter that will fit on the machine onto the arbor and crank up the arbor elevating wheel until as much blade is exposed above the table as possible. It may be necessary to flip back or totally remove the guard so that you have easy access to the side of the blade.

Now, you have to position the indicator point so that the point is perpendicular to the side of the blade and touching the blade as near the table as possible. The lower on the blade you go, the larger the blade gets in the horizontal dimension, but you have to be careful not to position it so that the side or back of the indicator housing touches the table or anything else. The dial indicator is so sensitive that any deviation in the table top will show up on the indicator and give you an erroneous reading.

Set the dial so that it reads zero, and you are ready to begin. Gradually slide the miter gauge along in the T-slot so that the indicator point travels along the blade body from just inside the teeth on the front of the blade to just inside the teeth on the back side of the blade. If the indicator reading between the two points is only .003″ to .005″, then your T-slot is essentially parallel to the side of the blade, and no adjustments are necessary. However, if the indicator reflects more deviation than you find acceptable, then you must get out your owner's manual and find out how to make this adjustment. As you are adjusting your machine, you will continue to use the indicator as just described to continually check and recheck as you are making your adjustments.

After you have the T-slot aligned, the fence needs to be adjusted parallel to both the blade and T-slot. The set-up is very similar to the one used to align the T-slot except the magnetic base is held against the fence and pushed along so that the indicator point travels along the same place on the blade. The magnetic base remains in the OFF position and the miter gauge is not used. *(Fig. 2)*

The difference in indicator reading from the front of the blade to the back is the amount the fence is out of parallel with the blade. There is some debate as to the best way to set a fence; some say that it shoud be dead parallel and others say that it should be slightly wider in the back than the front, but everyone agrees that the fence should *never* be tighter in the back than in the front. However you decide to set your fence, the indicator will let you see exactly what you have and help you make your adjustments to get it the way you want.

Once you have a little practice setting up the indicator to check your fence parallelism, you can make this check in about sixty seconds from start to finish. Since it is so easy to do, anytime you suspect the fence may be misaligned or you are about to cut an expensive piece of veneer ply, you can whip out the dial indicator and assure yourself that the fence is adjusted as you want.

If your blade guard has a splitter that must be aligned directly behind the blade, either the set-up that aligned the T-slot or aligned the fence (only if you have adjusted the fence exactly parallel to the blade) can be used to adjust the splitter so that it remains in the saw kerf. You simply move the indicator from the side of the blade (where you have set the dial to zero) on back to where the indicator point runs onto the side of the splitter. The indicator should give a reading that means the blade sticks out wider by a given amount than the splitter does. *(See Fig. 3)* The reading, when the point is on the front of the splitter, should be very nearly the same as the reading when the point is as far ack on the splitter as you can get it. This means that the splitter is essentially parallel with the blade. As an added check, you can flip the indicator set-up over to the other side and take the same indicator readings. The difference between the side of the blade and the side of the splitter should be about the same from both sides, assuring that the splitter is not only parallel but also centered to the blade.

FIG. 5: *Checking saw blade runout. The indicator point is touching the blade just below the gullets.*

FIG. 6: *Adjusting the blade parallel to the carriage travel. The indicator point is just below the blade flange.*

After making these three adjustments, you should get cleaner, more accurate cuts and have a greatly decreased chance of kickbacks because the wood will not get bound or pinched between the blade and the fence or splitter.

Radial Arm Saw

The radial arm saw is not only one of the most difficult machines to align but also one of the most difficult machines to keep aligned. To make matters worse, even slight misalignment on a radial arm saw shows up in the quality of cut it

makes and the increased tendency it has to 'grab and come at you'. Before we get into the specifics of the machine itself we will go over the procedure for checking blade and arbor runout.

The guard and blade must be removed to expose the arbor and blade flanges. The magnetic base is left in the off position and is set on the table in front of the arbor. The indicator shaft is adjusted so that it is perpendicular to the face of the flange. The point should touch the rim of the flange which would touch the blade body if there were a blade mounted. *(Fig. 4)* The arbor is rotated and the variation or runout is the total amount the indicator needle moves during one revolution of the arbor. It is much better, if possible, to rotate the arbor shaft by turning the opposite end from the arbor (the right hand end) so that the deflections you cause by putting your hand on the arbor will be somewhat removed from the indicator point. If the total indicator runout (T.I.R.) is .000″ to .0015″, your flange is probably about as true as you are going to get it. If the T.I.R. is greater than .002″, the runout in the flange is going to cause the blade to wobble noticeably at the rim. If the flange has unacceptable runout, it may be caused by bad bearings or a worn and sloppy flange.

Next, turn the indicator around so that the indicator shaft is perpendicular to the side of the arbor and the point touches the arbor just in front of the flange where there are no threads. Again, spin the arbor and notice the T.I.R. If it is more than .002″, you have a problem, maybe bad bearings or a bent arbor.

There is no need to try to get the blade to run true or in alignment if the arbor itself is not going to run true.

You can use this procedure to check the trueness of other items around the house such as lawnmowers, electric motor shafts, car wheel bearings, etc.

FIG. 7: *Setting a miter angle using a 'master' board. The guard is made of aluminum so the base is held in place with a parallel clamp.*

FIG. 8: *Testing Band Saw Wheels for runout. The magnetic base is attached to the frame wherever convenient and the magnet is 'on'.*

To check this alignment, the indicator base is positioned just about the same as when you were checking for the blade runout, except the indicator point should touch the blade body just a bit under the flange. *(See Fig 6.)*

The carriage should start out somewhere about the middle of the arm and then it is moved in and out to where the point of the indicator is ready to jump off the rim of the blade. The difference in indicator readings between the front reading and the back reading is the amount that the carriage is 'twisted', throwing the blade out of parallel with the travel of the carriage on the arm. A total deviation of .002″ is about the most that is acceptable while still obtaining optimum cutting results.

An additional check that is very handy for someone who uses their radial arm saw for precision mitering is adjusting the miter angle using the dial indicator. To do this, you need, in addition to the dial indicator, a standard or master board that contains the exact angle that you are trying to match with your radial arm saw miter adjustment. *(Fig. 7)*

To begin, you move your arm miter adjustment as accurately as you can to the desired angle. The magnetic base is securely attached to any convenient location on the carriage (or even the guard) with the magnet on. The point is touching and perpendicular to the mitered end of the master board while it is in place against the back fence. The carriage is moved causing the indicator point to travel along the end of the mitered master board. You can then adjust your machine and redo this check until you get miter adjustment to match the master board as accurately as you desire.

Band Saw

The band saw is a relatively straightforward machine and doesn't require many adjustments using a dial indicator until something goes wrong. Then, the dial indicator will be an immense help at either identifying the problem or eliminating something that you suspect to be the problem.

Now that you have satisfied yourself that your arbor is running true, you can check the runout on the saw blade. Mount the blade back on the arbor as you normally would and move the indicator base as shown in *Figure 5*. The indicator point is positioned perpendicular to the blade and the point is touching the blade body just inside the tooth gullets. Again, rotate the blade and read the T.I.R. for the blade rim. If you have a reading of much less than .010″, your blade is probably running about as good as you are going to get it. However, if the reading is .015″ or more or if the cut you get from the sharp blade is unacceptably rough, you probably have a blade with too much runout. The solution is to get a better blade.

After you have a blade that is running true, you can make the adjustment that is the most difficult to make and maintain. We are going to use the indicator to make sure that the blade is exactly parallel to the carriage travel as it is pulled out of the arm. If even the slightest deviation exists in this adjustment, it will cause the blade to 'heel'—the back side of the blade is cutting on one side of the saw kerf or the other, causing splinters and chipout, and an increased tendency of the blade to 'grab' and climb.

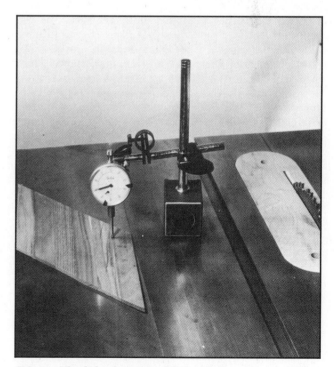

FIG. 9: *The dial indicator as a height gauge.*

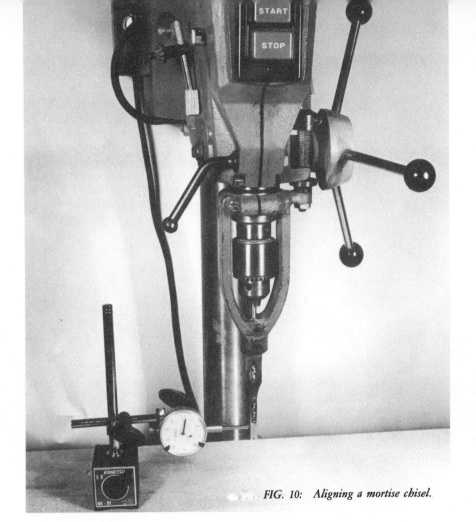

FIG. 10: *Aligning a mortise chisel.*

you let go of the indicator shaft end, the dial will read the thickness of the wood in thousandths of an inch. In the same manner, you can check to see if both ends or both sides of a board are the same thickness, or what the difference is. If you are trying to put a taper in a board, the indicator used as a height gauge will tell you exactly the taper you have achieved.

The same indicator setup easily converts to a depth gauge to check how deep a recess or groove is. Simply turn the magnetic base off when it is in the height gauge configuration and set it on the surface of the wood being measured with the indicator point down in the groove or recess. It may be necessary to adjust the indicator assembly lower to get the indicator point to touch and get a reading off of the bottom. The indicator base is moved so that the point is touching the same surface that the base is on, and a reading is taken. The reading from down in the groove is subtracted from the surface reading, and the difference is the depth of the recess.

The dial indicator enables you to get away from the measurement system that uses things as 'scant 1/16' and 'heavy 3/32' to one where veneer thickness may be .035", .040", .062", etc. and is much easier to work with.

If the band saw vibrates excessively or keeps throwing blades off the wheels, it is time to check for vibration and runout in the wheels. The guards need to be removed and both wheels need to be indicated on both the periphery and the sides. Attach the base magnetically any place handy on the frame and out of the way of the secure wheel. Adjust the indicator so that the point is touching and is perpendicular to the surface being checked. *(Fig. 8)* Turn the wheel slowly by hand and notice the variation in the indicator reading in one complete revolution. It helps to make a mark on the wheel to determine one revolution and to turn the lower wheel while indicating the upper wheel, and vice-versa, to isolate the runout of the wheel from variations caused by your hand as you turn the wheel. Do this to both wheels. On the sides or diameter of a band saw wheel where the T.I.R. is .005" or less, that wheel is probably not the source of the problem.

In addition to checking the wheels, you may have to pull the bad wheel and use the indicator on the shaft that turns the wheel. If there is runout in the shaft, the shaft may be bent or the bearings may be shot. By using the dial indicator as an investigative tool, you can identify the problem with a high degree of certainty before you begin tearing apart your machine and purchasing replacement parts.

Height Gauge

Many woodworkers have purchased a dial indicator and used it excessively as a direct reading height gauge. Many times in marquetry and other veneer work, it is necessary to know *exactly* how thick a piece of wood is or how deep is a recess.

By attaching the magnetic base to the top of a table saw or any other smooth ferrous metal surface and pointing the indicator point square into the table *(see Fig. 9)*, you have a direct reading height gauge when you reset the dial to zero. You can now lift up the point using the opposite end of the indicator shaft from the point and insert under it a piece of wood (or anything else that fits). When

Hand Router

The problem of vibration and rough cuts in the portable router is often caused by bent router bits. Even a slight bend or runout of .005" has serious implications in a tool that is turning 18,000 to 24,000 RPM (which translates to 300 or 400 revolutions per second). Again your dial indicator will help you identify the problem and point you in the direction of a solution.

The router is easier to work with if it is clamped upsidedown on the edge of a work bench top. The magnetic base is attached to a handy metal surface or C-clamped to the table. The indicator is adjusted so that the point is touching and perpendicular to the cutting edge. The reading that is produced as each cutting edge is rotated past the indicator point is compared to the reading from the other edge (or edges). A deviation of .002" is going to cut rough, and .004" or more is going to cause vibration.

Mortiser

The hollow chisel mortiser, be it a single purpose machine or an attachment for the drill press, usually needs more attention to alignment than it gets. Since it is not moving at a high speed like a saw blade, people must figure that close enough is good enough. The dial indicator can help you align your mortising chisel to produce cleaner cuts and to work smoother and freer.

The trick is to get the center line of the hollow chisel parallel with the travel of the chisel as it enters the wood. To complicate things, it must be remembered that most hollow chisels are taper ground; they are bigger down near the cutting edges than they are nearer the top.

To check for chisel alignment, attach the base magnetically to the drill press table or column and adjust the indicator so that it touches the chisel on the side being checked down near the cutting edge. *(Fig. 10)* Now, crank the chisel down until the indicator point is at the top of the chisel. Because the chisel is tapered, the indicator will reflect that the side indicated is some number of thousandths out of parallel. Before you make any adjustments, flip your indicator set up around and do the same check to the side opposite the side that was just checked. If the chisel is aligned perfectly, the indicator will show that the taper causes the same amount of deviation on two opposite sides. A difference in this deviation of .005″ to .010″ is probably acceptable, but any more than this means that the chisel is angled too much toward the heavy side. The other two sides must also be checked in the manner just described.

When the entire chisel is in proper alignment, in theory, the only part of the chisel that is touching the wood is right at the cutting edges. The rest of the chisel sides are relieved so that they offer no drag or resistance to the chisel being pushed through the wood.

Setting Knives in Shapers or Moulder Heads

The dial indicator is the only reliable method for setting two or more knives in a head at the same height that most of us can master. Not only can we get the knives running true and balanced for safety, but we get much smoother cuts because each knife is taking the same size chip as every other knife. *(Fig. 11)*

You go about achieving this desirable aim by putting the head in whichever machine is going to run it and attaching the indicator base by whatever means necessary in some handy location near the head or collars. The indicator is positioned so that it touches the outer edges or sides or whichever part of the

FIG. 11: Adjusting knives to the same height and diameter.

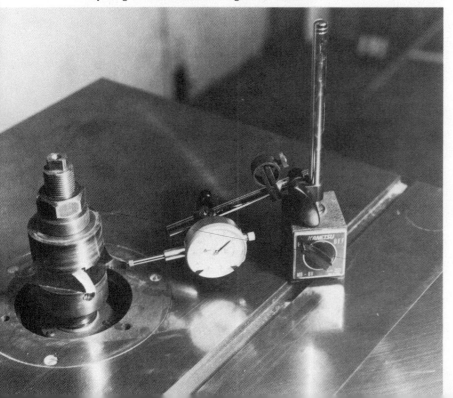

knives is being checked. As the cutter is rotated, you should get the same reading on all the knives during that particular measurement. Remember, the indicator point must glide up onto and across the cutting edge so the cutterhead must be rotated backwards, causing the indicator point to approach the cutting edge from behind. Quite often you will have to lift the indicator point by using the end of the shaft opposite the point and lower it onto the bevel relief at the approach of the cutting edge. This assures that you don't lose accuracy in your setup and maybe even permanently damage the indicator itself by having the point or stem bang against a shoulder or protrusion.

Particularly, the two or three wing moulder heads that are made to use insertable knives to cut moulding on a table or radial arm saw have to be indicated at least two places on the knives. If they are set evenly on the diameter, they may still be staggered from side to side; so they have to be set accurately on the side also. Don't get too frustrated trying to get them exactly perfect because they were not made for as tight a tolerance as you can measure with your dial indicator. In that case, your indicator will enable you to set your head to at least the accuracy to which it was originally manufactured and to also see how far from perfectly accurate that is.

So, in summary, we can agree that the dial indicator earns its keep and your favor in the following ways: Machines are set up and aligned to meet or exceed original factory accuracy. Difficult operations can be performed because the machine and entire cutting system are operating at the optimum. Safety is increased because some causes of accidents have been eliminated and others have been reduced. Machine maintenance and repair will be much simpler because you will have diagnosed the problem before beginning. And, finally, the intrinsic joy of woodworking is greatly increased because the tools you use will be doing exactly what you have them do and the finished product will reflect only your workmanship and not imperfections caused by inaccurate cutting tools.

About The Author:
Thomas W. Miller is a woodworker living in Winchester, VA. He operates Precision Grinding Company. He also wrote "Setting Jointer Knives", The American Woodworker, Sept. 1985.

Making Your Own Tools

by Nicholas Cavagnaro

Few pleasures bring as much satisfaction as using a tool that you have made yourself. This is especially true if the tool is well made and even more so if your creation is not available in the marketplace. The making of tools, however, is surrounded by much mystery, legend, and alchemy, confounding most people into believing that it is only for the experts. This is plainly not so and the ability to make tools is a great advantage to the craftsman seeking solutions to special tasks.

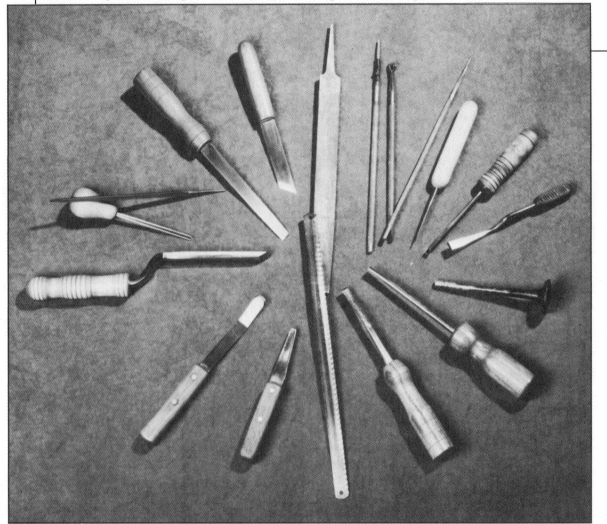

(Clockwise from hacksaw blade): razor knife (from hacksaw blade); cranked bullnose chisel (from hacksaw blade); cranked neck paring chisel (from truck leaf spring); veining tool (from triangular file); straight carving chisel (cold ground from file, then tempered; note the washer to prevent the handle from being split when the chisel is struck with a mallet); skew chisel (cold ground from file, then tempered); old flat file; chainsaw files; dovetail scriber (ground from chainsaw file tang end); 3/16" bevel edged chisel (from chainsaw file); small cranked neck chisel (from chainsaw file); automobile valve; screwdriver (from round file); gouge (ground from automobile valve.

Steel is without a doubt one of the greatest inventions achieved by man. Despite its low cost and the neglect with which we treat it, discarding tons of it everywhere, no metal can match the value this material has added to our lives. Of special interest to the craftsman wanting to make his own tools is high carbon steel. High carbon steel is temperable, meaning that it can assume many different combinations of hardness and springiness brought out by the use of heat. High carbon steel is everywhere. It can be found in springs, old screwdrivers, old files, old sawblades, old knives, and many other articles. Most of the tools I have made started out as old files. Files have a very high carbon content and can produce some of the best edge-holding tools. One of my finest carving gouges is made from an old automobile engine valve. Its edge is keen and has held up under thousands of mallet blows in some of the toughest woods. Despite the addition of various alloys to high carbon steel to create "tool steel", you will still be able to temper it. High carbon steel is unmatched for its ability to take and hold a very fine edge when properly tempered.

In order to temper high carbon steel, it must first be hardened. This is accomplished by getting the metal cherry red hot. Use an old pair of pliers for tongs. The color has to go all the way through the metal. If you can see a darker spot in the middle, it is not hot enough. Small tools can be formed in the flame of a propane torch. I have made many small carving knives, chisels, and scribers using the combined flames of two small propane torches. Larger tools require a forge to provide enough heat for the hardening process. A forge is simply a fire with forced air on it to supercharge the fire and provide more heat. The old way of providing forced air was with bellows. Today you can achieve the same with a vacuum cleaner, sticking the hose in the exhaust end. The simplest forge I have used was a barbecue with briquets for a fire and my son holding the vacuum exhaust hose while I worked the metal. I have also made tools in a large blacksmith's forge with coke for a fire and with an automatic blower built into the forge. Most of the tools you will make yourself will be small and can be heated by the propane torch method or by the barbecue and vacuum cleaner method when the occasional need arises.

Once the steel is cherry red all the way through, you must quench it. Water works alright but quenches very fast and has a tendency to warp the steel. Most of the time I quench in a coffee can full of used motor oil. This provides a slower cooling but still produces a good hardening on small tools. However, do it outside. Lots of smoke will be produced when you thrust the hot steel into the oil. There is always the possibility of a fire, though I have never gotten anything more than the small flicker of a flame once or twice. If you quench in oil in your shop, you will not be working in your shop for a while because it will be full of choking smoke.

Now that you have quenched the steel you are ready to temper it. First check to see if you have hardened the steel properly. Try an old file on it. If it glances off and won't cut, you've hardened your steel. Now polish the steel with some fine sandpaper so you will be able to see it change colors when you heat it again. The finer you shine it the better you will be able to detect the finer hues that will appear. Heat the tool with a propane torch, moving the tool around quite a bit and heating the thicker parts more than the thinner parts. The first color that will appear is straw, then bronze, peacock, purple and dark blue. Straw is for fine knives or chisels that will be used with care. Bronze is for heavier duty chisels or knives. Peacock is for thin springy tools. The more you draw the temper the more you relish hardness and gain springiness, unless you go beyond the

This is a skewed paring chisel. The bevel is ground from each side so the cutting edge is in the middle. This way it can cut right or left. This chisel was made by cool grinding a file, then termpering out some of the hardness and brittleness. The tool handle is walnut.

dark blue color, in which case you have annealed or softened the steel. Tempering also relieves stresses in the steel that were captured or locked in during the hardening process. When you get the color you want, cool the steel immediately to prevent the tempering process from continuing beyond where you want it to stop. Water or oil is fine for cooling. You will find that tempering is the trickiest part of tool making. The heat must be applied carefully so as not to overheat the thin parts before the thicker parts get hot enough. If you go past the color you want to stop at and get your tool too soft, you will have to harden it again and re-temper it. As your skill progresses, you may wish to temper the various parts of the tool differently: harder at the cutting edge, springier toward the handle.

I left out a discussion of how to shape your tools until I had first described the hardening and tempering processes. Generally you will want to rough shape your tool before hardening it. You can anneal it to make it easier to grind. Anneal by getting the steel hot enough to turn it blue and let it air cool slowly. Annealed high carbon steel can be hacksawed, drilled, and filed. You can shape the steel with a hammer and anvil or bend it into various shapes if you get it cherry red or even a little bit hotter (dark yellow). You do not want to work your tool too much into a finished state before hardening because a crust forms during the hardening process and some pitting of the surface often occurs. You can also expect some warpage or distortion. At one time I made a hunting knife. I annealed the steel first, then carefully shaped and ground it until I had a beautiful knife. Then I spent hours polishing with various grades of wet or dry sandpaper and water until it was the most delightful and graceful thing to behold. I proceeded to heat it in a forge, but when I quenched it in water, it warped. I heated it again and hammered it flat, marring my beautiful polished finish, before quenching again. Still it warped. I heated and hammered again and the next time I quenched it, it cracked! So invest your time in doing the fine shaping work after you get past the hardening phase.

A disc sander works much better for shaping than a grindstone. It cuts faster and with less heat, as long as the sandpaper is sharp. You can do some of the finest flattening and polishing work with wet or dry silicon carbide paper on a flat surface using water as a lubricant. You can also flatten and polish on an oilstone or waterstone. I usually rough shape before hardening, final shape before tempering, then fine polish, flatten, and sharpen after tempering. Just remember that after you have hardened the steel, you cannot let it get so hot that you draw the temper while working it.

Tools can be made from files without going through the hardening process. However, you cannot get the file too hot while working it, otherwise you will draw the temper. If you hand hold it while shaping on a disc sander you will not let it get too hot since the tempering process takes place at over 400ºF! Just be especially careful when grinding fine edges. Keep a can of water near by to cool it off every now and then. Since you can't work the steel in an annealed state with this method, it is slower going and your sanding disc will get duller faster.

Since files are harder and more brittle than any tool you will want to make, all you need to do once your tool is shaped is draw the temper to the proper color for the use you have in mind. This method works best when you start out with a file that is pretty close to the shape of the tool you are wanting to make.

The tool in the foreground is a small cranked neck chisel made from a chainsaw file. I used two propane torches together to provide heat for shaping and the hardening process. The handle is walnut with notches cut in it for gripping the small handle. The tool in the background is a 3/16" bevel edged chisel, also made from a chainsaw file. The handle is curly maple.

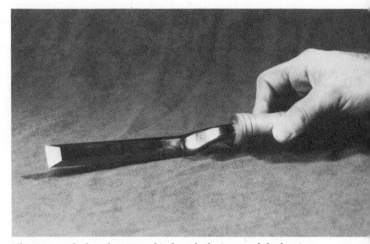

This is a cranked neck paring chisel made from a truck leaf spring. I used a forge for heat. The handle is birch.

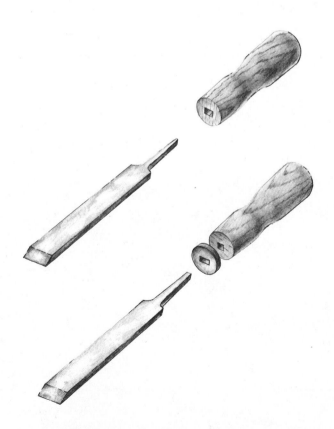

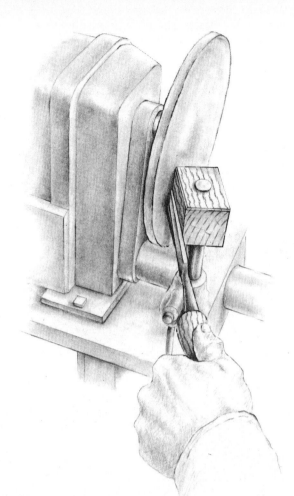

For handles, design your own to fit your hand. You can turn them on a lathe or carve them. Drill a hole for the tang to go in and glue it in place with epoxy glue or epoxy putty. It should be a tight fit, necessitating that you hammer the handle on the last bit of the way or drive it home in a large vise. However, don't have it too tight or force it so much that the handle splits. Fancy metal ferrules are not necessary on either end of your tool. Walnut, ash, maple, and birch make very good handles. So will many other woods. When a handle wears out you can always replace it. Crush the old handle in a steel jawed vise. Then heat the tang to remove any remaining epoxy as long as you don't get it so hot that you start to draw the temper. The epoxy will soften long before it gets that hot.

For a heavy duty handle that will be struck with a mallet most of the time, make sure the end of the tang isn't pointed so that it cannot be driven up into the handle. A better way to insure that the tang doesn't get driven further into the handle is to fit a metal disc or washer in place between the junction of the handle and the blade. The disc should fit tightly so that it will lock the blade portion against the base of the handle and keep the tang from going into the handle when the handle is struck.

Jig for grinding standard chisels and plane irons on a drill press with a horizontally spinning grinding disc or sanding disc.

This jig fits in the tool rest holder of a lathe. It aligns a chisel or plane iron for grinding the bevel with a sanding disc. Adjust the jig in the tool holder so that you grind a 25° bevel.

Screw on a strip of metal to hold the bottom edge of the blade horizontally. Flat back of blade goes against wood block.

Steel shaft approx. 6" long to fit in tool rest holder. Get a long bolt the right diameter and cut if off.

Screws will lock the block to the steel shaft. Drill a small hole or file a flat place on the shaft.

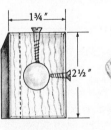

1¾"

2½"

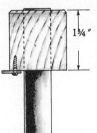

1¾"

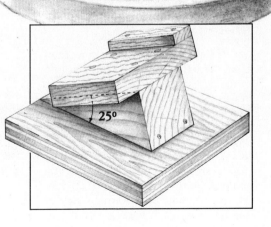

25°

CROSS SECTIONS

The cross sections of tools will vary according to the intended use. When making chisels, use the following general guidelines. For all purpose work select a bevel edge. This will allow for undercutting. The bevel edge will also sharpen easier since there is less material to remove. It can be used for light work with a mallet, but should be thought of as a hand powered tool. For heavier work such as chopping, the firmer chisel shape can be used. It contains more steel than the bevel edge and will stand more abuse, especially when using a mallet. The heavyweight champion is the mortise chisel. It is designed for heavy chopping. The sides of the blade "ride" the mortise, insuring a uniform width of cut. While these examples have been given for chisels, the principles can be applied to other types of tools you might try to make.

TIP ANGLES

To measure the angle you want to grind on a tool, you can use a protractor to draw the angle on paper or you can set an adjustable bevel gauge to the chosen angle. Now you must devise some way to help hold the tool while grinding so that you will get this angle. Rests can be devised in all sorts of ways to suit your particular grinding equipment. Just make the rest solid and keep it as simple as possible. Some home-made jigs are illustrated here.

The ground bevel is usually 5° less than the honed bevel. After grinding, hone on an oilstone or a waterstone. This is followed by stropping on leather charged with buffing compound (jeweler's rouge) or by buffing on a charged wheel. The reason the ground angle is less than the honed angle is that it makes honing easier—you have less steel to remove with your oilstone or waterstone.

To get a chisel really sharp requires that the back be honed truly flat and smooth. I have found the best way to do this is with a large diamond stone (such as sold by Garrett Wade) or with wet or dry sandpaper on a piece of plate glass using water as a lubricant. The diamond stone is by far the best and the high cost ($100) is not so bad when you realize that the diamond stone doubles as the ultimate sharpening stone. It always stays flat, it needs no lubricant, it cuts extremely fast, and never wears out. It also re-flattens any sharpening

stones you have with no damage done to the diamond stone. The Garrett Wade catalog also contains some of the clearest and most detailed information on sharpening that I have found.

Some people hone the bevel with a jig and some don't. I prefer a jig because it is fast and gives razor-sharp edges with no rounding over. The best jig for honing is, in my opinion, the Precision Honing Guide made by Lee Valley Tools of Canada. Garrett Wade sells it along with several other honing guides. All the different jigs and guides work, but the Lee Valley guide is precision made and built to last.

Below is a table giving some important grinding and honing angles. The angles don't have to be exact. For harder use on the tool and for cutting harder wood, the angle needs to be a bit greater. For fine hand held and hand driven cutting tools the edges can be ground and honed a bit finer.

TOOL	GRINDING ANGLE	HONING ANGLE
Standard chisel	25°	30°
Mortise chisel	30°	35°
Plane iron	25-30°	30-35°
Paring chisel	20°	20-25°
Gouge*	25°	25°

*Gouges are usually ground and honed at the same angle. The inside edge is also honed.

In the future when you need a special tool that can't be bought, make it yourself. With experience you will gain confidence and skill, and may even get to the point where you feel that your best tools are the ones you make yourself.

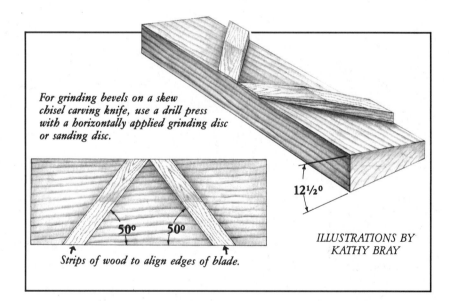

For grinding bevels on a skew chisel carving knife, use a drill press with a horizontally applied grinding disc or sanding disc.

12½°

50°   50°

Strips of wood to align edges of blade.

ILLUSTRATIONS BY KATHY BRAY

For more information, write for the Garrett Wade Catalog, 161 Avenue of the Americas, New York, NY 10013, cost $4.00. Information may also be obtained from *The Making Of Tools*, Alexander G. Weygers, Van Nostrand Reinhold, 135 W. 50th St., New York, NY 10020; *Tools And How To Use Them*, Albert Jackson and David Day, Alfred A. Knoph, New York, NY; *Woodshop Tool Maintenance*, Beryl M. Cunningham and William F. Holtrop, Charles A. Bennett Co., Inc., Peoria, IL 61614.

ABOUT THE AUTHOR:
Nicholas Cavagnaro is a professional woodworker in Orofino, Idaho.

Tool Cabinet

by Dennis Watson

Proper storage and care of fine tools

are essential to insure they are sharp, true and accurate.

Photos by Dennis Watson

Imagine your good chisels rattling around in a drawer with screwdrivers, hammers, pliers, etc.; they're going to become nicked and dull. In addition, tools should be conveniently located next to the workbench so they can be easily reached and put away when you're through with them. A wall-hung cabinet seems to be the answer.

Adjustable shelves provide storage for large items such as a router, drills and sanders. The doors are deep enough to efficiently install holders for chisels, squares and screwdrivers, and the drawers provide storage for additional small items.

Before I decided on the dimenstions of the cabinet, I made a layout of the tools I wanted to store in it. Since your tool collection is probably different than mine, I suggest you lay out where the tools will go and alter the dimensions if necessary.

Box joints seemed like the appropriate way to join a cabinet, especially one being used to store woodworking tools. Box or finger joints are easily cut on the table saw using a dado blade and are very strong because of the large gluing area. Rip the stock for the top and bottom (A) and sides (B) of the case 8 inches wide, and the top and bottom (C) and sides (D) of the doors 2½ inches wide, then crosscut to length.

To cut the box joints, you'll need to make a jig for the miter gauge which supports and spaces the board to be cut (Photo 1). Install a ½ inch dado blade in the table saw and cut a ½ inch wide by 1 inch deep slot in a 4 × 12 inch scrap piece of plywood. Glue a hardwood block ½ inch

Photo 1. *Box joints are easily cut on the tablesaw using a ½ inch dado blade and a shop made jig. Attach sandpaper to the jig to prevent the wood from slipping.*

Photo 2. *To cut the box joints, slide the board tightly against the stop block and make the first cut. Place the cutout over the stop block and cut the second cutout. Continue in this manner to finish the joint.*

wide, 1½ inches long and 1 inch high in the slot. Clamp the jig to the miter gauge with the spacer block exactly ½ inch from the dado blade. Before you screw the jig to the miter gauge, cut a box joint in a scrap piece of wood; more than likely you'll need to adjust the spacing a little to get a good fit. When the spacing is correct, screw the jig to the miter gauge. Glue rough sandpaper (about 150 to 180 grit) to the jig to prevent the board from slipping.

The male end of the joint is cut by pushing the board tightly against the spacer block and cutting the first slot. (Photo 2). Slide the slot over the spacer block to set the distance for the next cut. Continue in this manner across the width of the board. The female end is cut by aligning the edge of the board up with the outside edge of the dado blade. After the slot is cut, the board is pushed tightly against the spacer block. The remaining slots or fingers are cut similar to the male end.

When cutting box joints, usually there is a fair amount of tearout on the back side. This can be minimized by knifing a groove along the back side of the board. (Photo 3). Also, a dado blade does not cut a perfectly flat bottom and you'll need to square the bottom with a sharp chisel after you have cut the joints. (Photo 4). Run a ¼ × 2³⁄₁₆ inch rabbet in the door top, bottom and sides. Be sure to stop the rabbet about 1 inch from the ends. (Photo 5).

When cutting box joints, usually there is a fair amount of tearout on the back side.

Dry fit the case and doors together to make sure the joints pull up tight. Add glue and clamp, making certain the case is sqaure by measuring across the diagonals. Allow to dry overnight. Run a ¼ × ⅜ inch rabbet in the sides, top and bottom of the case for the back with a rabbet bit equipped with a pilot guide.

Rip the divider (E) 7¾ inches wide and crosscut to length.

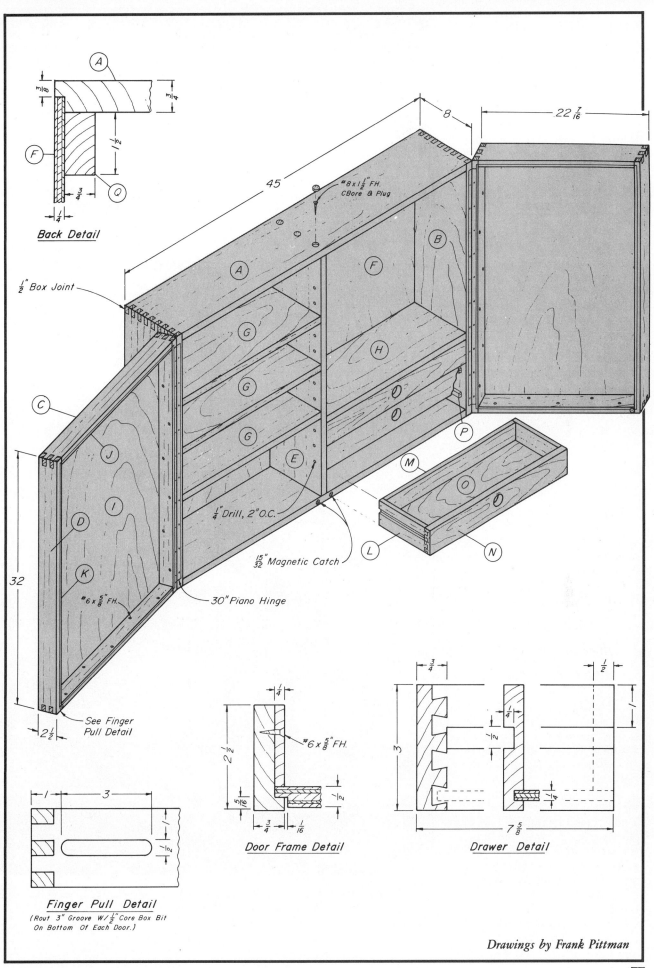

Back Detail

½" Box Joint

45

#8 x 1½" F.H.
CBore & Plug

8

22 7/16

A

B

F

A

F

G

H

C

G

G

J

E

I

D

K

¼" Drill, 2" O.C.

15/32" Magnetic Catch

30" Piano Hinge

#6 x 5/8" F.H.

See Finger
Pull Detail

32

2½

P

M

O

L

N

Finger Pull Detail

(Rout 3" Groove W/ ½" Core Box Bit
On Bottom Of Each Door.)

Door Frame Detail

#6 x 5/8" F.H.

Drawer Detail

Drawings by Frank Pittman

Clamp in place, then drive three No. 8 × 1½ flat head screws in each end. Counterbore the screw holes and fit with plugs cut from scrap. (Photo 6). Cut the back (F) to fit, then tack or screw in place.

Rip the adjustable shelves (G) 7¾ inches wide and crosscut to length. Drill ¼ inch holes on 2 inch centers in the sides and the divider. Screw the fixed shelf (H) in place similar to the divider.

Cut the plywood front (I) from ½ inch oak plywood, then run a ⁵⁄₁₆ inch wide by ¼ inch deep rabbet around the edges. The front is made from ½ inch plywood because more than likely you'll want to screw attachments or holding blocks to the panel and ¼ inch plywood would not be thick enough.

Rip the stop 1 ¹⁵⁄₁₆ inches wide from ¼ inch oak and crosscut the top and bottom (J) and the sides (K) to length. Install the door panel and screw the stop in place with No. 6 × ¾ inch flat head screws.

Cut a ½ × 3 inch finger pull in the bottom of the door with a router and ½ inch core box bit. (Photo 7). The doors are attached to the cabinet using a continuous hinge. First, motise the case and door to accept the hinge, then screw the hinge in place.

I joined the drawers together using dovetails cut with a router and template

The drawers are the next order of business. First, rip the side (L) 3 inches wide and the back (M) 2½ inches wide from ½ inch oak and crosscut to length. Rip the front (N) from ¾ inch oak and cut to length. I joined the drawers together using dovetails cut with a router and template, but an alternate joint could be used. (Photo 8). Run a ¼ × ¼ inch groove in the sides and the front for the ¼ inch plywood bottom (O) and a ¼ × ½ inch groove in the sides for the drawer slides. Glue the drawer together using the bottom to keep it square. After the glue has dried, tack the bottom to

Photo 3.   *To reduce splintering when cutting the box joints, scribe a line on the back side of the board the thickness of the wood, then knife the scribe line a little deeper.*

Photo 4.   *Since a dado blade does not produce a flat bottom cut, you can square and clean up the rough cut with a ½ inch chisel cut from both sides.*

Photo 5. Cut the rabbet in the door frame using the router table and a ½ inch straight cutter. Several passes will be required to finish the rabbet.

the rear using small brads. Drill a 1¼ inch hole in the front for a finger pull. Be sure to round over the edges.

Rip the drawer slides (P) ½ inch wide from ¼ inch oak or maple. Attach a piece of double backed tape to the slide, then slide the drawer and slide in place. Remove the drawer. The tape will hold the slide in place. Permanently screw in place using three No. 6 × ¾ inch flat head screws. Rip the hanger strip 1½ inches wide, crosscut to length, and glue to the top of the case.

...I used walnut because it contrasted nicely with the oak

Finish the cabinet as desired. I used two coats of Watco Natural Danish Oil with the second coat wet sanded using No. 600 wet / dry paper. Drill the holes for the round magnetic catches and install.

For tool holders, I used walnut because it contrasted nicely with the oak, and I attached them with flat head brass screws.

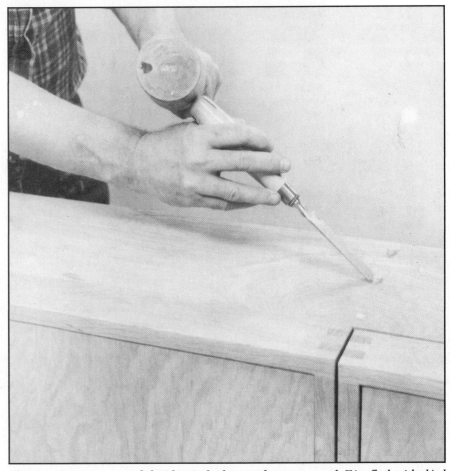

Photo 6.   Screws are concealed with ⅜ inch plugs cut from scrap wood. Trim flush with chisel and sand.

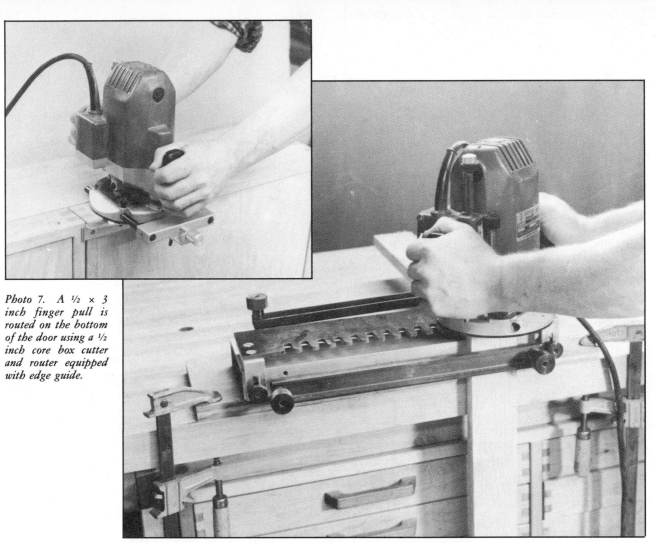

Photo 7. A ½ × 3 inch finger pull is routed on the bottom of the door using a ½ inch core box cutter and router equipped with edge guide.

Photo 8. The drawers are joined together using a dovetail joint. The joint is easily and accurately cut with a router and dovetail jig.

TOOL CABINET CUTTING LIST

Key	No.	Size	Material	Description
A	2	¾″ × 8″ × 45″	oak	case top and bottom
B	2	¾″ × 8″ × 32″	oak	case side
C	4	¾″ × 2½″ × 22⁷⁄₁₆″	oak	door top & bottom
D	4	¾″ × 2½″ × 32″	oak	door sides
E	1	¾″ × 7¾″ × 43½″	oak	divider
F	1	¼″ × 31¼″ × 44¼″	oak plywood	back
G	3	¾″ × 7¾″ × 21¼″	oak	adjustable shelf
H	1	¾″ × 7¾″ × 21⅜″	oak	fixed shelf
I	2	½″ × 31″ × 21⁷⁄₁₆″	oak plywood	door panel
J	4	¼″ × 1¹⁵⁄₁₆″ × 31½″	oak	stop top & bottom
K	4	¼″ × 1¹⁵⁄₁₆″ × 20¹⁵⁄₁₆″	oak	stop sides
L	6	½″ × 3″ × 7¼″	oak	drawer sides
M	3	½″ × 2½″ × 20⅜″	oak	drawer back
N	3	¾″ × 3″ × 21⅜″	oak	drawer front
O	3	¼″ × 6¾″ × 19⅞″	oak plywood	drawer bottom
P	6	¼″ × ½″ × 7″	oak	slide
Q	2	¾″ × 1½″ × 21⅜″	oak	hanger strip

ABOUT THE AUTHOR:
Dennis Watson is a contributing editor to The American Woodworker.

Mortising Jig

by Pat Warner

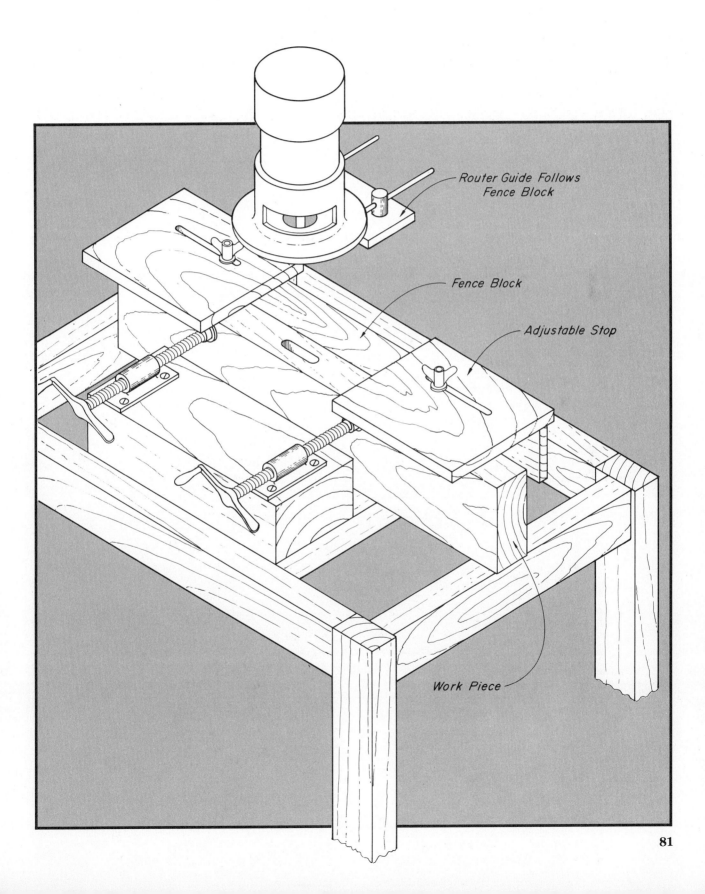

Router Guide Follows
Fence Block

Fence Block

Adjustable Stop

Work Piece

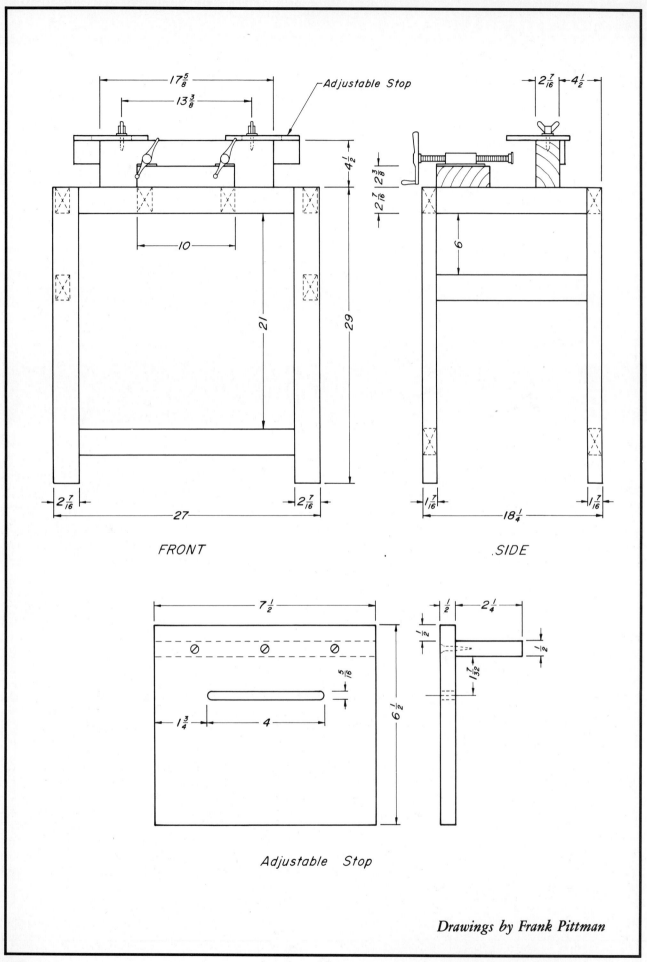

$17\frac{5}{8}$

$13\frac{3}{8}$

—Adjustable Stop

$2\frac{7}{16}$ $4\frac{1}{2}$

$4\frac{1}{2}$

$2\frac{3}{8}$

$2\frac{1}{16}$

10

6

21

29

$2\frac{7}{16}$

$2\frac{7}{16}$

27

$1\frac{7}{16}$

$1\frac{7}{16}$

$18\frac{1}{4}$

FRONT

SIDE

$7\frac{1}{2}$

$\frac{1}{2}$ $2\frac{1}{4}$

$\frac{1}{2}$

$\frac{1}{2}$

$1\frac{7}{32}$

$\frac{5}{16}$

$6\frac{1}{2}$

$1\frac{3}{4}$

4

Adjustable Stop

Drawings by Frank Pittman

This fixture, along with a router, make mortising a snap. The fixture consists of a table like frame, a strong fence, two press screws which hold the workpiece in place, and two adjustable stops (slides). The adjustable stops and the router edge guide define the four walls of the mortise.

Once the fixture is set up for a particular mortise, the edge guide and slides will insure that all successive mortises will be the same. The router I use, a B&D #3310, allows easy rack and pinion settings, and I can cut mortises with it in one to two minutes to depths of ¾″ - 1 1/8″.

The fixture consists of a frame with four legs and a pair of beams tenoned into the top long rails to which a block fence is dadoed and bolted. The frame members are cut from 6/4 ash and net 2½″ x 1 7/16″. The block fence measures 2 7/16″ x 4½″ x 17 5/8″ and is bolted down with 6½ x 3/8 carriage bolts. Its location is 4½″ from the side rails. Two 5/16″ x 2″ hanger bolts are located on the block on 13 3/8″ centers centered on the block. These hanger bolts with washers and wing nuts fix the adjustable stops and keep them parallel to the block.

...stops are made of ½″ hardwood & slotted...

The adjustable stops are made of ½″ hardwood and are slotted so they slide parallel to the block. Since the router base rides against the ends of the stops they must be squared up well so that

the resultant pathway of the router yields the ends of the mortise parallel. The slots in the slides are 5/16″ wide and 4″ long and therefore slide 4 inches.

The press screws (model PS-9S from Adjustable Clamp Co.) are bolted to the cross beams on a pillow so that when fully opened the pads are 3½″ from the block. This distance and the distance between the underside of the stops and the block holding beams constitute the maximum cross section the fixture will accept (any length is acceptable). Mine measures 3½″ x 4″.

To use the fixture, first scribe the mortise on the stock and locate its long center midway between the press screws and clamp in place. Set the right and left hand stops against the router base by locating the straight faced router bit to cut inside the scribe lines. Set the edge guide to cut the side of the mortise as referenced off the press screw side of the fixture. Lock stop collars on the guide bars so this position can be located again for the next mortise. Next, cut this section to depth (which is only one cutter width). Now set the edge guide so the cutter will reach the far side of the mortise and set another set of stop collars on the guide bars for this adjustment. Now, route the remainder of the mortise to depth.

ABOUT THE AUTHOR:
Pat Warner is a designer and furniture maker from Escondida, Ca.

Variable Jig for Cutting Tapers

By W. Curtis Johnson

Whenever you need two nonparallel rip cuts, the variable taper-cutting device will come in handy. It is probably most useful for sawing tapered table legs, but it can also be used to make jigs for sawing the pins and tails of through dovetails. To make the device you will need two pieces of 1 x 3 at least 24 inches long, a narrow two inch hinge with screws, two 1/4 by 4 inch carriage bolts, two washers, two nuts, a wing nut, and some scrap hardwood. The two pieces of 1 x 3 must be dry, straight, dressed smooth, and cut to equal lengths. Construction is illustrated in the figure.

Drill a hole for a carriage bolt in each board about two inches from one end and parallel to the end through the 3 inch width of the board. Cut a notch 1/4 inch deep on one side of each board and wide enough to accomodate the head of the carriage bolt. Put the two boards side by side with the notches together and attach the hinge to the other end.

The crossbar should be made of scrap hardwood about 1 and 1/2 inches wide and eight inches long. Drill a 1/4 inch hole 3/8 of an inch in from one end. Rout, or drill and file a 1/4 inch slot to within one inch of either end of the board. This slot will provide the adjustment.

The board riding against the fence will contain the fixed bolt and the other board will be variable. Glue a block of hardwood to the outside of the variable board to serve as the stop for the board to be cut. This stop must extend about 3 inches in from the end to avoid cutting the crossbar when the blade is high. Glueing is preferred over screws in case the blade cuts into the block. Actually, the block may have to be sacrificed for certain cuts and may have to be replaced from time to time.

When the glue is dry, seat the two carriage bolts in their holes and add the crossbar. The crossbar will have to be rounded at the fixed end so it doesn't hit the fence. Put one washer on each carriage bolt and add the two nuts to the fixed bolt. When they are snug but still allow the crossbar to

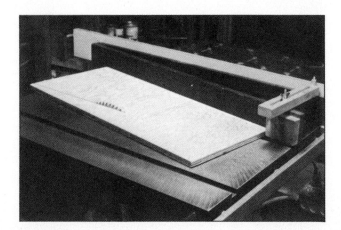

move, tighten the two nuts against each other. Put the wing nut on the adjustablt bolt. Adjust the device for the appropriate angle.

The photo shows the variable jig cutting a taper on a circular saw. The blade guard has been removed for clarity. The fixed side of the jig moves against the fence, and with one corner against the stop the work moves with the variable side.

Although I took the photo on my circular saw because it shows the use of the device more clearly, I really prefer to rip on my little band saw. If the blade is sharp the bandsaw consistently rips a straight line using the fence. Woodcraft bandsaw blades seem to come sharp. I've had to sharpen the few other bandsaw blades I've purchased to avoid wandering and having the blade lead the cut.

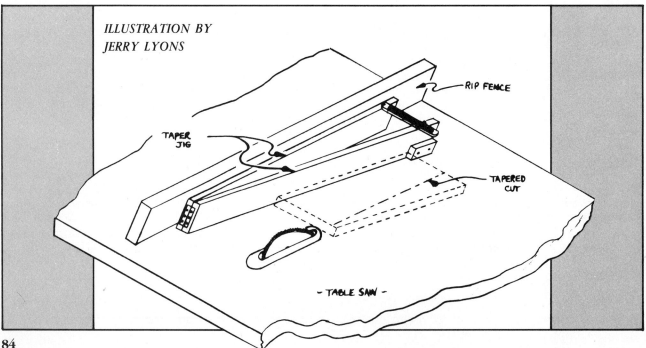

ILLUSTRATION BY JERRY LYONS

RIP FENCE

TAPER JIG

TAPERED CUT

- TABLE SAW -

Earlier this year I received an order to build three doors for a hotel in my home town. The doors were to be built of 1¾″ thick oak. In order to facilitate handling the heavy oak timbers while sawing, jointing, and drillpress mortising, I designed and built a set of roller supports for my shop. My shop is small and compact, so I did not want to have a couple of free-standing roller supports to store. The solution I came up with was to make two roller supports that can be clamped to my sawhorses or to my workbench. When not in use, they store conveniently on the wall and do not occupy valuable floor space.

The construction of each roller support is very simple. The post upon which the roller and its mounting assembly is attached is made of a piece of 2 x 4 softwood. The roller and its mounting assembly should be made of hardwood for strength. I turned my rollers from birch and used cherry for the horizontal piece and the two side arms. The steel pins upon which the roller turns are cut from steel spikes and driven into holes drilled in the end of the roller. If you don't have a tight fit, use some epoxy to secure them. Finish the roller with paste wax and leave the other parts unfinished.

To use the roller supports you will probably have to nail a piece of 1 x 6 across the legs on the end of your sawhorses so you will have something to clamp to. Then all that is necessary is to clamp the roller supports at the right height for the task you are doing, whether it be sawing, jointing, or using your drill press. My workbench is located behind my tablesaw, so I clamp one roller to the edge of my bench with a couple of long bar clamps when I need to saw long lumber. I also position one roller support in front of the saw, attached to a sawhorse, to help me hold the long lumber and roll it forward into the saw. When jointing long lumber, I have a roller support attached to a sawhorse on each end of the jointer. If your sawhorses are lightweight, you may wish to weigh them down with a few bricks or other heavy objects to stabilize them when the rollers are clamped in place.

The best part of all is that when I am not using the roller supports, they hang on my wall without taking up floor space, yet are ready to be of service whenever required.

ROLLER SUPPORTS FOR YOUR SAWHORSES
by Nicholas Cavagnaro

ABOUT THE AUTHOR:

Nicholas Cavagnaro is a professional woodworker in Orofino, Idaho.

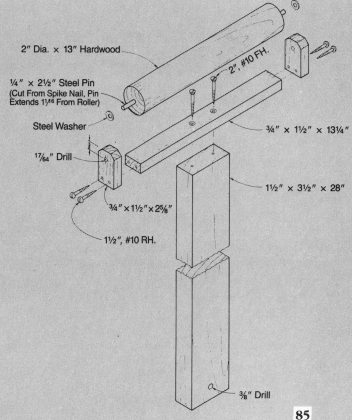

2″ Dia. × 13″ Hardwood

2″, #10 FH.

¼″ × 2½″ Steel Pin (Cut From Spike Nail, Pin Extends 1¹/₁₆ From Roller)

Steel Washer

¾″ × 1½″ × 13¼″

¹⁷/₆₄″ Drill

1½″ × 3½″ × 28″

¾″ × 1½″ × 2⅝″

1½″, #10 RH.

⅜″ Drill

Large Diameter Caliper For Turning

by Scott D. Emme

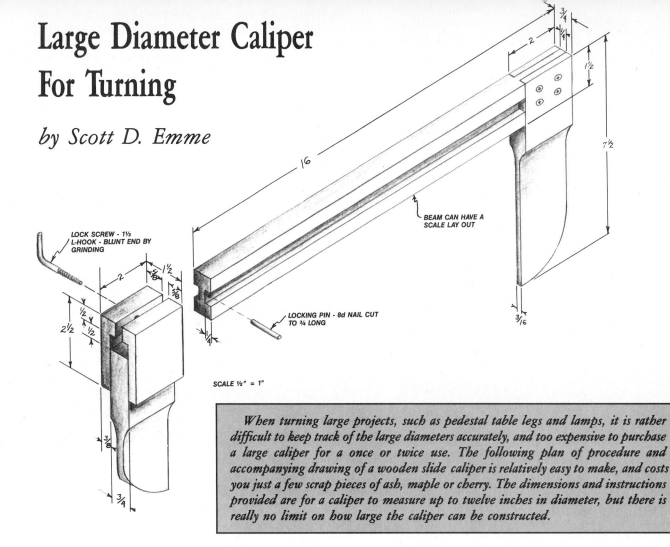

LOCK SCREW - 1½ L-HOOK - BLUNT END BY GRINDING

LOCKING PIN - 8d NAIL CUT TO ¾ LONG

BEAM CAN HAVE A SCALE LAY OUT

SCALE ½" = 1"

> When turning large projects, such as pedestal table legs and lamps, it is rather difficult to keep track of the large diameters accurately, and too expensive to purchase a large caliper for a once or twice use. The following plan of procedure and accompanying drawing of a wooden slide caliper is relatively easy to make, and costs you just a few scrap pieces of ash, maple or cherry. The dimensions and instructions provided are for a caliper to measure up to twelve inches in diameter, but there is really no limit on how large the caliper can be constructed.

To construct the beam:

1. Cut a piece ¾" x 1½" x 16" long.
2. Cut a groove on both faces of the stock; ½" wide and ¼" deep and ½" from what will be the bottom edge of the beam.
3. Cut a tenon on one end of the beam for the solid head to be attached. The tenon should be ¼" thick by 2" wide.

To construct the solid head:

1. Cut a piece ¾" x 2" x 7½" long.
2. Cut a through mortise on one end, leaving a gap ¼" wide by 1½" deep.
3. Resaw the other end to form a long tenon of about 5" in length and 3/16" thick. The cut can be coved at the end as pictured.
4. Secure the head to the beam with glue and #6 x 5/8" flat head screws.
5. Check for accurate squareness between the head and beam.

To construct the adjustable head:

1. Cut one piece ¾" x 2" x 6½" long and two pieces 5/8" x 2" x 2½" long.
2. Resaw a tenon on the 6½" piece; leaving a 3/16" x 5" tenon as described in step three of the solid head construction.
3. Cut the two 2½" pieces into an "L" shape; leaving a lip ¼" tall and ½" wide. (This lip should fit the grooves of the beam.)
4. Glue the adjustable head together, sandwiching the 6½" piece in the center as shown. (Be sure to leave a ½" space between the 6½" piece and the lips cut on the 2½" pieces.)
5. Once the glue is set, make any necessary adjustments and/or cuts to allow the head to slide smoothly in the beam grooves.
6. Drill a pilot hole through one side of the head's lip and install a 1½" L-hook for a set screw to lock the head in place when using. (Grind the point of the L-hook flat to prevent splitting the beam.)
7. To trap the adjustable head on the beam, a pin may be installed in the groove on the open end. The pin may simply be made from a ¾" length of an 8d nail; driven through a slightly smaller diameter hole.

To finish the caliper, a coat of danish oil may be applied. A ruler may also be marked on one face of the beam to allow quick, easy measurements to be made on large diameter stock.

Dust Collection System

By Rick Williams

It takes only about a minute in a shop with no dust collection system to understand how important an effective dust collection system is. Unfortunately, it only takes a minute with a price catalogue to discover why so many shops do without. I was faced with a shop which could generate enough dust in 10 minutes to take an hour to clean up. When I moved my shop to commercial space I was determined to keep it clean by developing a dust system which would handle all my dust collection needs. I could not afford to have a big fancy commercial system, so I built by own.

I had been trying to defeat demon dust in my home shop for years, and consequently had acquired a Bell Sawdust blower, which I had found to be completely inadequate for anything but the lightest applications. In my efforts to find the true meaning of a clean floor I discovered that W W Grainger had high pressure blowers of good size at a good price. I bought a 1hp direct drive blower for about $200.00 and that was 90% of the battle right there.

When I moved the shop to commercial space, it was time to upgrade the dust system, and get all of the machinery on one or two systems. We are now collecting from two shapers, a radial arm saw, an 8'' jointer, a resaw, and a 20'' planer. Since I have a two man operation, we seldom have more than one machine running at a time. Through the use of shutoff valves at each machine we are able to maintain maximum air intake volume at each machine thus assuring maximum effectiveness at each machine. The blower will handle more than one of the lighter dust producers at a time, but the planer must operate on it's own. As the shop is now, the system is effective. When we grow to larger size, we may go to a double blower system.

The principle components to my dust control system are a 1 hp, direct drive high pressure blower, 6'' galvanized tubing, plastic plumbing parts, scrap wood, scrap formica, and the all important duct tape.

The blower is literally the heart of the system. I use a high pressure blower with self cleaning veins. It is important to have a blower that can handle solids in high volume without clogging. Also the blower must be able to handle large volumes of air at increasing static pressure with minimum loss of efficiency. There are blowers which will handle more air initially than a high pressure blower, but their efficiency drops far faster as pressure increases. A radial vein blower may move 3 times as much free air but will deliver about the same volume at 2'' of pressure as a high pressure blower of the same power will at 6'' of static pressure. This is very important as the pressure of the system will increase as the filter medium clogs.

The next key component in my dust system is dust confinement. Since I didn't want to heat the great outdoors, I wanted to trap the dust, filter and return the air to the shop. I did this by buying about 10 yards of canvas and sewing it into two bags, one on the blower and one in reserve. The canvas does a remarkable job of filtering the air. I know there must be small particles in the air, but the area surrounding the dust bag shows very little accumulation of dust from syhat I had expected. The bags can each hold one and one half to two

The heart of the system. A 1 HP direct drive blower.

Close-up showing a homemade shut-off valve.

cubic yards of dust and shavings. We have come close, but never filled a bag in one day. Usually we only need to change the bags once or twice a week.

As the bag fills with dust it will progressively decrease the amount of filter surface available to the system. This causes an increase in the static pressure inside the bag. Increased static pressure decreases air flow volume and thus system performance. It is best to empty the bag on a regular basis and not wait until the bag is completely full, and performance downgraded.

Once you have a blower and a bag you need to have a place to put it and a way to get it hooked up to the machines. I placed mine in the least useful corner of the shop. It takes about 16 square feet of floor space. Since it is some distance from the machinery, I wired it with a double pole single throw 24V/240V relay and wired the low voltage circuit to two three way switches which are located in fairly handy locations. To connect the machinery to the blower the least expensive thing I could find was 6'' galvanized duct. Most important in your layout is to make sure to restrict air flow as little as possible from each input point. Avoid unnecessary turns and reductions in hose size as these will downgrade performance of the system. Each opening in the system must be able to be closed off when not in use to optimize performance at the machines which are in use. The principle shut off method we used in our system was made from scraps of plywood about 8'' square with 6'' diameter holes in their centers. The two pieces are placed face to face with their holes aligned, and shims about 1/8'' thick to hold them apart enough so that a piece of plastic laminate can be easily slid between them to block the holes. The pieces are then nailed together on opposite edges through the shims. A flange can then be attached on opposite sides and the valve inserted in line, wherever it is needed.

My machines are grouped together in clusters based on usage and required space. We built a wooden box about 4' tall and ran several gates off of it. We also incorporated a floor sweep trap into its base. It has since been dubbed R2D2 by my brother-in-law. As far as individual machine hook-ups go, if there is a factory hook-up available, use it. If not, use your imagination, tin snips, pop rivits, scrap wood, duct tape and plastic plumbing parts. The most important thing to make sure of is that you do not interfere with the operation of the machine or any of its safety equipment.

A combination of parts including the shut-off valve, flexible hose, plastic tubing and galvanized tubing.

A floor sweep trap incorporated into the dust system.

Galvanized tubing connects the blower to the equipment.

The collection system can be placed in an "out of the way" location.

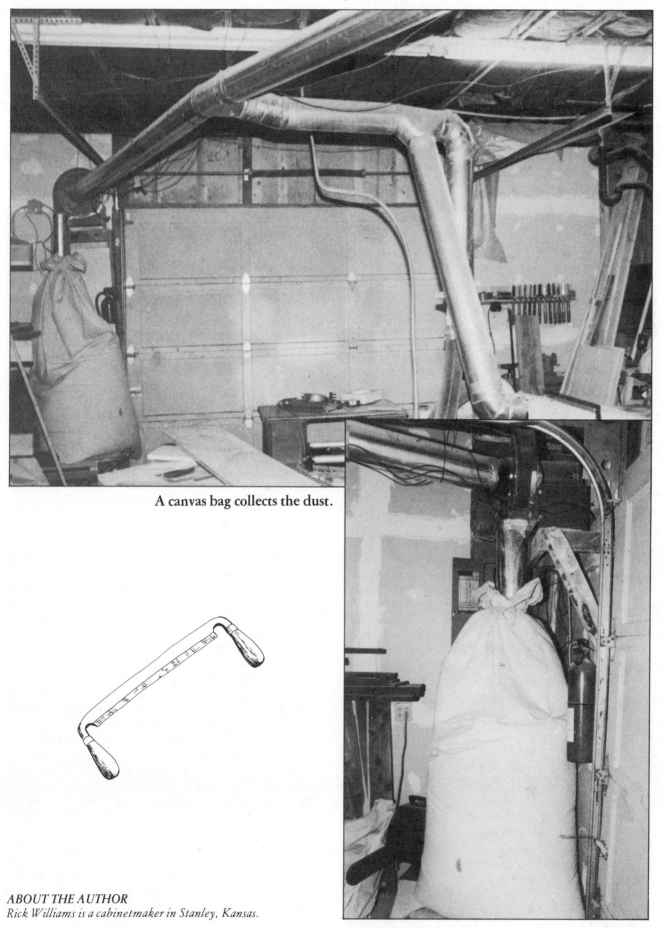

A canvas bag collects the dust.

ABOUT THE AUTHOR
Rick Williams is a cabinetmaker in Stanley, Kansas.

The Finishing Room

Some Key Elements To Consider

by Mac Campbell

Finding proper conditions to apply a slow drying finish is a problem which has plagued woodworkers since the invention of varnish. Today's varnishes, polyurethanes and other relatively slow drying finishes, can produce a tough, durable and attractive finish if properly applied, but all the skill and work in the world can be wiped out by air borne dust settling into the still wet film. The only solution when this has happened is to scrape, sand, and try again, often with the same results, until finally the entire finish winds up scraped, sanded, and tediously hand polished with rottenstone. While hand rubbing remains the final step in a first class finish, the finishing room set-up described here can significantly reduce the work required.

Most finishes cure by a solvent release process; the film dries and hardens as the solvent evaporates into the surrounding atmosphere. For this to happen most efficiently, there must be a steady, gentle flow of fresh air over the piece being finished. This, of course, is easy to arrange; any fan will do the trick. (To test this, varnish a scrap and place it directly in front of a fan. The drying time will be surprisingly short.) Unfortunately, this system almost guarantees a dusty, unacceptable finish. The successful finishing set-up, therefore, must have the capacity to move *filtered* air over the drying film. In addition, this air should be warm, as this tends to encourage evaporation. For those of us in northern climates, a minimum amount of heat should be lost to the outside during the finishing and curing process. Finally, while a facility for spraying such highly volatile finishes as nitrocellulose lacquers may well be beyond the capacity of the typical woodworker, it would be nice to be able to spray the lower volatility finishes (e.g. the new water based lacquers) and some stains.

The finishing room described here meets all of these requirements at a cost of under $100.00. In my shop it is installed in an 8′ x 16′ room which has a common wall with the main part of the shop. The system is based on two used furnace blowers. Blower #1 is simply mounted in an outside window in the finishing room. When required, the window is opened and a plywood baffle is used to block off that part of the window not filled by the fan. The fan is controlled by a switch outside the finishing room. Air to replace that exhausted by the fan enters the room from the main part of the shop through a double thickness of furnace filters mounted in the wall between the shop and the finishing room. While this fan is in use, a window in the shop must be opened to avoid

Blower #1. Plywood baffle to right of blower can be removed and the window closed when not in use. Filter bag for blower #2 is in the background.

creating a partial vacuum in the shop and filling it with smoke from the furnace.

Blower #2 is mounted on the ceiling of the shop, and feeds air into the finishing room through a duct. (In my shop, I covered the space between two ceiling joists with 1/8″ plywood and used the resulting enclosed space as the duct.) The air leaves the duct in the finishing room and passes through a filter bag salvaged from a commercial dust collection system. (The polyester fleece used to line clothing works admirably as a dust filtering medium, though it should be backed with cotton or canvas for strength.) Since the windows in the finishing room are closed when this blower is in use, the air in the finishing room returns to the shop through the furnace filters mounted in the wall, and no heat is lost.

Lighting in the finishing room is provided by three strips of flourescents, each consisting of one cool white and one warm white tube. (I have tried the "daylight" tubes, and I find the combination of warm and cool white gives a better color balance.) In addition, there is a south and an east facing window, providing plenty of natural light. One additional feature that is useful, particularly if you do not happen to have good natural light, is an incandescent light on a movable pole fixture. Finishes are best checked for flaws by looking at their reflection of a light source, and the light from flourescents is too diffused to be effective for this purpose.

Blower #2. Enclosed ceiling joists serve as a duct.

any spraying involves these liquids unless otherwise informed in advance. All of these factors should be thoroughly checked before proceeding with setting up the finishing room.

Because I already had a compressor in the shop, it seemed only natural to run an air line into the finishing room. With a transformer (a combination pressure regulator and moisture trap) mounted on the finishing room wall, I can regulate the pressure while in the room. This has given me access to the broad range of lacquer-based stains now available. (I get mine from Mohawk Finishing Products, Amsterdam, N.Y., and St-Leonard, P.Q.) These stains must be applied by spraying because they dry almost instantly. Because they are so fast-drying, they can be used quite successfully on different woods to make colors more uniform. They are, for instance, ideal for staining Windsor chairs made with the traditional combination of ash, pine, and maple. Where an oil based stain would penetrate the three woods differently and emphasize their differences, the lacquer based stains tend to make the color more uniform while still allowing the figure of the wood to show through. Applied with an air-brush, these stains are also excellent for blending in the sapwood of walnut where the light color would be objectionable.

The finishing room has proven a valuable addition to my shop facilities. It has broadened the range of finishes I am able to apply successfully and doubles as a storage area for partially completed pieces. An unexpected bonus has been its use as an "air conditioner." By wiring a clock timer switch to blower #1, setting it to run between 2 and 4 a.m., and leaving a window open in the far end of the shop, I can fill the shop with fresh air during the coolest part of the night. Since the shop is in the basement, that coolness holds through the hottest part of the following day.

One final note. If you live in a city, various building and environmental codes may regulate how much, if any, vapor and/or spray you can exhaust to the outside. In addition, there may be restrictions on what types of material may be sprayed without being equipped with explosion-proof lights, switches, fans, etc. Check with local authorities before going ahead. You should also check with your insurance agent; many policies, even commercial ones, do **not** cover spraying and/or storage of highly volatile liquids, and the insurance company may assume that

Double thickness of washable furnace filters in wall between shop and finishing room.

Air transformer, mounted on finishing room wall. Extra air outlet to left of transformer powers blowgun for final dusting prior to applying finish.

ABOUT THE AUTHOR:

Mac Campbell is a professional woodworker living in New Brunswick. He owns and operates a custom woodworking shop.

SHOP SAFETY

By Bill Marsella

To the homeworkshop enthusiast the shop is probably the one place in the world where stress of the business day stops at the shop door and a period of contentment awaits inside. The one place in the world where a man or woman can create, maturate, and do the things that they want to do, not what the community expects them to do. But with all its attributes the homeworkshop can be a most dangerous place. The machinery and tools that it contains can cause severe lacerations and the environment can be laden with toxic fumes, dust, etc.

Certainly we are cautious. We depend upon both training and diligence to avoid injury and one would imagine that this would suffice. Yet accidents happen anyway. How? A little investigation will reveal that the accidents that threaten us are many times built into the shop when we put it together. These facets will be discussed here.

The shop as a recreational facility — The shop is the one place in our daily life that offers us respite from the stresses that most of us have to tolerate in our daily lives. We seem to react then in a manner that suggests that since this area can be the oasis of contentment that we are therefore, safe. We then tend to relax our defenses and it is this insidious mentality that leaves us prone to injury. The frequency of accidents tends to attest to this.

Further, the average craftsman gravitates to his shop at the end of the day, a time when he is normally fatigued and this certainly is not the time to face challenging situations. As a comparison, the accident rate in the commercial sector increases with the hours worked (as men tire) and this we can understand, yet in a like situation, the homeworkshop, we seem to overlook the same measure when applied to our own activities. As we become more fatigued we have to depend more heavily upon our reflexes to maintain a margin of safety in the face of the situation wherein the machinery that we use is just as unforgiving as that utilized in the commercial sector. So just as in the commercial sector, the possibility of an accident increases proportionally with the degree of fatigue that we sustain.

Training and experience — When dealing with a recreational facility it seems that "if we can afford it, we can do it." This makes no sense of a ski slope, for instance, and makes even less sense in the home workshop. We have been raised in a mechanized society and anything that can be done, can be done on a machine. To the veteran woodworker the fallacy of this statement is clear but not everyone has attained that degree of expertise. This classification of craftsmen chooses tools and machines carefully and knows the difference between tools that are labeled "craftsman" or "home utility." Tools are designed to perform definite levels of performance and they should be used accordingly. If a tool is used in the manner in which its designer intended, it is usually a safe implement but this can also apply to an automobile. Few of us have to be reminded of the consequences of the misuse of this machine; the same view can be assumed for the tools in the home workshop. Lacking experience and training, the home workshop enthusiast sometimes pushes his tools and machines past the designed safety parameters and an accident is the result. The accompanying photographs (using the table saw) are an example. This machine is found in almost every shop, is extremely versatile

Our author in his shop.

and a safe tool to use when used properly. The pictures illustrate how (too often) expediency and lack of training over-rides good sense.

To begin with, the guard (blade) has not been used for such a long time that it can no longer be found. Not only will this safeguard protect the operator from lacerations or dismemberment but kick-backs and material thrown in the face of the operator as well. As an example, when carbide blades are misused they heat (as any blade will that is not sharp or used properly) and the brazing that holds the tips to the blade can fail. These tips can leave the edge of the blade with the speed of a bullet. I grind many of these blades for carpenters and many times the carbide tips are missing! On the shop bench saw, one with the glade guard missing, this blade damage could have resulted in a serious, if not fatal, accident.

Another important thing, a safety precaution, is that blades on a bench saw must be sharp and properly set all the time. Saws, for the operation and material worked, must be in perfect condition, otherwise they tend to get hot. An overheated blade can fracture at any time. Now maybe it will, and then again maybe it won't, but why take the risk?

Without the blade guard and splitter assembly (the kick-back claw is usually part of this assembly) kickbacks are guaranteed! On narrow pieces, the slightest misalignment at the end of the cut and the teeth of the blade will grab the work and send it directly into the direction of the operator. The velocity of this is so violent that it is comparable to the speed of a hunting arrow. The work will easily pierce aprons and clothes, burying itself into the groin of the operator. It does not require a large commercial machine to do this, an 8'' blade will do nicely. In the photograph you will notice that the operator is standing on the side of the centerline of the blade. Standing in this position is the only safe way to use this machine. What can happen — will!

The lathe is a wonderful machine and since I was a teenager I must have spent hundreds of hours working on it. It is truly a fascinating machine, yet used in a careless manner it is extremely dangerous. Heavy pieces, larger than what the machine was designed for, have a habit of leaving the machine without permission! The tail stock tears out of the work first and the part comes flying out of the machine in the direction of the operator. On a small machine this is like being hit with a baseball bat, but on an over-taxed large machine this accident could be fatal. Not too long ago I was turning some picture frames (outboard) and the work fractured in the machine; one piece took out an eight foot fluorescent light and the other crushed itself against the wall. No notice of impending diaster — just an explosion-like sound, instantly! This reminded me of an accident that I had on my first lathe when I was a teen-ager. I had yet to learn that when turning slender pieces that the work must be supported at the center to eliminate whipping and bowing of the piece being worked. My lesson was quick and decisive — the piece was thrown from the machine and hit me square across the forehead, knocking me to the floor! I was fortunate on this one, the only thing that was hurt was my pride. No idler (mid-centers), no face mask, probably dull chisels, and the minimum of training — the perfect prescription for an accident.

The economics of the shop — Notwithstanding experience, it seems that the amount of money that we have to equip a shop is another facet that reflects itself on the hazards of the shop. In order to save money, too often tools and machines are used or altered to perform tasks that they never were designed to do. Years of experience in my shop have taught me that each tool is designed for a particular purpose and to alter (jury-rig) any machine is inviting disaster. We seem to be quick to demand that the commercial sector maintain strict conformance to safety standards, while creating conditions quite the opposite in the home workshop.

We buy machinery, the best that we can afford, and then tend to use it as if it was industrial quality machinery for a large furniture factory. The worst offense that we are prone to is to under-power our machinery. We don't deliberately do so, but we do anyway because that is all the power that we have to use. When a saw, for instance, is under-powered, a series of complications occur. Lead in wiring becomes hot, this heat increases the resistance in the wire, the power requirement is then heightened further. If we do not burn out, or shorten the life of the windings, we encourage the possibility of a fire. How often do you turn on your saw and the lights flicker or dim momentarily (nearly always!) When a motor labors it turns at a slower RPM and consequently the periphery speed of the blade is reduced. The blade, taking longer to get through the cut heats up, inviting a possible mechanical failure (fracture) of the blade, dulling, and possibly the loss of the carbide tips. But we have found a way to compensate for this — we 'tease' our way through the cut before we blow a fuse and this does work (it's done every day) but we have to spend so much attention to get the piece cut that our attention is divided from the care that is required to use the saw in the first place. One moment of lost concentration and — the rest is hind sight!

Shop space and location is another factor that seems to build hazards into the workshop. Again, we do not do this by design, we use all the space that we can afford but machines are not known for their charity. Unless there is sufficient room to operate them safely, they stand ready to remind us at any time. For example, setting a machine near a water pipe is sheer suicide. Unless the machine is perfectly grounded, and I've seen few that are, particularly direct drive saws, any connection (you for instance) between the machine top and the water pipe provides a perfect ground. I saw a home owner prove this one day when he was using a skill-saw while framing an attic room. He was standing near the vent stack that ran from the first floor through the attic and the roof and inadvertantly bumped against the stack as he was cutting a piece of framing material. He almost went into cardiac arrest, instantly, and can thank the EMT who came in sufficient time to save his life.

The third prong on outlet plugs is there for a reason — yet more are cut off than are left intact because an adapter is not handy. Incidentally, an adapter is of limited use unless the pig tail on it is mechanically grounded to an outlet box that is itself grounded to the system.

Fire is always waiting in the wings when it comes to the work place and no where is it more prevalent than in the home workshop. Again, in industry we demand that fire exits, extinguishers, prompt fire protection, fire blankets, etc. exist, yet how many home workshops have even a fire extinguisher in the shop? When a shop is in the basement (usually near a boiler room) the hazards waiting are considerable.

The commercial sector has particular problems that don't exist in the home workshop—don't that is, if furniture stripping and lacquer is not used. In one wood shop in which I was the shop superintendent, I instructed the finishing foreman to discard all rags and waste that were used for filler and lacquer each day in a drum outside of the plant. I was concerned about spontaneous combustion and a plant fire. The foreman methodically conformed to this order each day and each night there was a fire in the drum in the yard. There was adequate ventilation and we were careful to leave the cover off the drum to be certain that there would be no build-up of fumes, but we had fires anyway. The only way that we solved this problem was to flood the drum with water over the level of the waste material inside. How many home workshops could withstand the scrutiny of a Fire Marshall.

Unauthorized personnel — The home workshop is suspect to a hazard rarely found elsewhere — people who shouldn't be there, are. Children seem to be the worst offenders. Some machines (radial arm saws is one example) have a switch that can be locked in the off position with a key but many machines do not have this safety feature (assuming of course that this feature is used *every time*). A router is a good example to use. Small enough to be handled by a child and designed to run at least 25,000 RPM it provides an attractive hazard for many. A regular 3/8'' drill is even a better example. Small, "harmless," and convenient, yet it has been the source of many electrocutions when used ungrounded and where conditions are damp or wet.

Space here does not provide the opportunity for a complete discussion on the dangers inherent in the home workshop; I have only concerned this writing with a few of the implements that are found there. Those of us with experience in this facility and who own fully equipped shops are infinitely concerned with the limitations of the equipment that we use constantly and even further, our own limitations; the latter may well be the more important of the two. We have worked in our shops (many of us since we were children) and consider ourselves fortunate to have this outlet of self-satisfaction. But with

Standing to one side of the center line of the blade is the only safe way to operate this machine.

each benefit there goes responsibility, care, training. It is these facets that will assure us of even more years of enjoyment in the home workshop.

The home workshop is probably the one place where a person can exercise the most freedom; freedom from the stress of the world around us, but unless care is exercised it can also be a very hazardous place to enter at the same time.

ABOUT THE AUTHOR
Bill Marsella is an Industrial Designer and woodworker living in Lynbrook, New York.

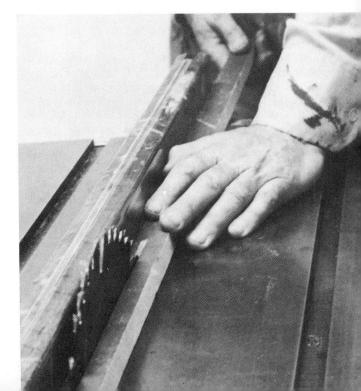

The slightest misalignment of the part in the cut will guarantee that this part will be thrown into the operators body.

Index